C000026976

FIRE AND ASHES

**How Yorkshire's finest
took on the Australians**

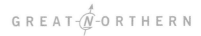

Great Northern Books Limited

PO Box 213, Ilkley, LS29 9WS

www.greatnorthernbooks.co.uk

© Great Northern Books Limited and contributors 2009

Every effort has been made to acknowledge correctly and contact the copyright holders of material in this book. Great Northern Books Ltd apologises for any unintentional errors or omissions, which should be notified to the publisher.

All rights reserved. No part of this book may be reproduced in any form or by any means without permission in writing from the publisher, except by a reviewer who may quote brief passages in a review.

ISBN: 978 1 905080 52 6

Design and layout: David Burrill
Printed and bound in Great Britain by Butler Tanner & Dennis Ltd, Frome, Somerset

CONTENTS

PREFACE

There are eighteen Yorkshiremen still alive who, whilst playing for Yorkshire, also participated in the Ashes Tests. In this book they recall favourite memories and stirring moments in their own words. Collectively they reveal how Yorkshire's finest took on the Australians in one of international cricket's most famous rivalries.

The memories go back to the early 1950s with Brian Close and Bob Appleyard, and range over the next half century up to the 2005 Test that included Michael Vaughan and Matthew Hoggard.

Published to coincide with the 2009 Ashes – and especially with the 4th Test at Headingley Carnegie Cricket Ground – it is appropriate that Yorkshire's 'field of dreams' should feature prominently in these pages. Geoffrey Boycott recalls Fred Trueman's superb action in the 1964 Test, while Ken Taylor and John Hampshire also contribute their special memories. But no book of this kind would be complete without Chris Old's account of the events of 1981 – 'the Greatest Test of all time, the Miracle of Headingley and the most unbelievable revival in fortunes in the history of the Ashes'.

The publishers gratefully acknowledge the help of Yorkshire County Cricket Club in the preparation of this book and also Yorkshire Post Newspapers for making photographs available.

England's Geoff Boycott celebrates reaching his century in his first test match for three years on July 30, 1977 (PA)

INTRODUCTION

GEOFFREY BOYCOTT

To be seen at its absolute best, I believe cricket must be a fair contest between bat and ball. The pitch and climate at Headingley nearly always provides that.

Too many surfaces are monotonously flat and boring. Sometimes even five-day Tests peter out into draws, and a handful of batsmen go home with hundreds. That's fine for their egos and their batting average, but not good for the spectators or the game of cricket. Headingley is different. I always say to players, 'Don't go looking for a draw there.' If the weather holds, it is a 'result' venue – pure and simple – so think positive.

It explains why Headingley has staged so many memorable and compelling Test Matches. Donald Bradman's phenomenal scoring over 20 years; Fred Trueman's 11 wickets against Australia in 1961; my own hundredth hundred in 1977; the 'miracle' of England's Ashes comeback there in 1981.

While Headingley's cloud cover often creates the right conditions for swing, the surface itself offers encouragement for a bowler too – but only if he bowls a full length. He has to use his nous. Headingley isn't the place to pitch short. If you bang the ball in, it tends to sit up nicely to cut or pull. There is no steepling bounce like Perth or Brisbane. But if you bowl a full length – well up to the batsman – the ball kisses the top and hurries off.

Fast bowlers used to come to Headingley and claim it lacked pace. In particular, John Snow, who bowled for Sussex at Hove, which was very pacy in the 1960s and 1970s. I remember sitting in the Headingley dressing room with him before the start of a Test. Snowy started to grumble about what he perceived as lack of speed in the Headingley pitch. Alan Knott interrupted him. 'But John,' he said, 'you always get four and five wickets whenever you play here.' He got them because he was smart enough to bowl the right way – a full length and on a consistent, accurate line.

But batsmen can score runs at Headingley too. Bill Bowes used to tell me about Bradman, who he bowled first ball in the second 'Bodyline' Test at Melbourne in 1932-33. Bill said that Bradman was incredibly nimble on his feet – quick and alert. Of course, he was an expert at almost every shot in the book, but cutting and pulling were two particular strengths. You need true bounce to be able to play those shots, which emphasises the nature of the Headingley pitch during the period in which Bradman scored 963 runs on it in six innings – 334, 304, 103, 16, 33 and an unbeaten 173 at an average of 192.60.

I've seen no better innings at Headingley than Peter Burge's against England in 1964. It was only my 2nd Test – and the first on my home ground. The Australians were struggling on 163 for five when Ted Dexter took the new ball and asked Fred Trueman to get rid of Burge and polish off the tail. Fred did take Burge's wicket – but only after he'd made 160!

With hindsight, it was the wrong decision to put Fred on. The spinners were bowling well and should have been allowed to finish the job. Burge was in exceptional form, and he played a full range of shots. When there's swing in the air, or seam off the pitch, bowlers need fielders in catching positions close to the bat. That leaves gaps to be exploited. Burge took advantage of those gaps hitting cleanly and stroking his way around the field. While the tailenders hung around Burgey took the game away from England in a superb display of positive stroke play. It gave Australia a decisive first innings lead of 121 runs and they went on to win the match comfortably.

Often younger people, who never saw Fred play, ask me whether he was truly fast. Believe me, he was – very fast indeed. He also did something that most other bowlers couldn't. During his best years Waqar Younis used to swing a full ball into the batsman at terrific pace. He didn't bowl short because he knew Headingley so well. Well, Fred could do it the other way, which is much harder to achieve. He always came in on a smooth run from the Kirstall Lane End, which was appreciably downhill back then.

As a boy, I was sitting on Headingley's hard wooden benches in 1952 when India lost four wickets for no runs to the first 14 balls of the Test. Fred claimed three of them in eight balls. He'd taken two of them when the chap sitting near us told my friends and I: 'If he gets another, I'll buy you all an ice cream.' When Fred did, the chap was true to his word.

I'll always be grateful to Fred for that ice cream!

Geoffrey Boycott, 2009

Geoffrey Boycott celebrates reaching his 100th hundred at Headingley in 1977 (YP)

Chris Old (YP)

CHRIS OLD

Born: December 22, 1948, Middlesbrough

After making his debut for Yorkshire at 17, he took 1,070 first class wickets at an average of 23.48. Had injuries not frequently frustrated him and his career, his figures would be even more impressive. He also scored almost 8,000 runs at 20.84.

Test record:	
Span:	1972-81
Matches:	46
Wickets:	143
Best bowling:	7-50
Average:	28.11
Runs:	845
Average:	14.82
Catches:	22

Headingley:
July 16, 17, 18, 20, 21, 1981

It's still called the Greatest Test of all time and the Miracle of Headingley – the most unbelievable reversal in fortunes in the history of the Ashes.

At the time, I honestly don't believe that anyone who witnessed it – either live on TV or at Headingley – could quite believe that we'd fought our way back from a succession of seemingly impossible positions to beat Australia in such dramatic, utterly implausible circumstances. In fact, I can tell you that most of the players on either team could scarcely believe it either. Afterwards, I was as stunned as the Aussies. Not until hours later – as I was driving down the M1 in the early evening – did I fully appreciate exactly what we'd done and how we'd achieved it. It simply hadn't sunk in before then. I heard the reports on the car radio and actually said to myself. 'No, we couldn't have won'.

The game itself is so well known that I hardly have to go through the fine detail of it. How Australia piled up 401 before declaring; how we were bowled out miserably for 174 and were forced to follow on; and then how we found ourselves on the brink of being crushed, on 135 for seven in our second innings, before Ian Botham began his belligerent, brilliant hitting to change everything. At one stage the bookmakers made us 500-1 to beat the Australians. More like 1,000-1 in our eyes. By rights, we didn't have a chance.

Headingley '81 will always belong to Botham, whose summer went through the extremes of professional triumph and disaster. The disaster came when he had to give up the England captaincy after losing the first Test and then drawing in the second at Lord's, where he also got pair. Botham had taken over from Mike Brearley. On form alone, he was the natural choice – 140 wickets and more than 1,300 runs, including six centuries, in 25 Tests. It proved to be the wrong move. He drew eight and lost four of his 12 Tests.

Of course, the triumph came at Headingley and then Edgbaston, and I was privileged to be part of it. But I have to admit one thing. I wouldn't have been in the team at all if Botham had still been skipper. I only got my chance at Headingley because Brearley was brought back in a last, desperate measure to save a series that we were in danger of losing badly.

My problems with Botham started on the winter tour of the West Indies. We disagreed over several things, and particularly his handling of Graham Dilley, who was still a month away from his 21st birthday and on only his second overseas tour. Botham wasn't good at dealing with the psychological aspects of captaincy. When Dilley bowled a few bad balls, or things didn't go well for him in the first Test at Trinidad, Botham's idea of dealing with it certainly didn't match my own. He started to take the micky out of Dilley. There were a string of leg-pulling remarks that Botham actually meant in a serious way. I could see that Dilley felt worse because of them. He took 0-73. Nothing Botham said was geeing him up. On the contrary, I could see, from his demeanour and his body language, that he was suffering even more.

I told Botham that he ought to be encouraging Dilley instead of making smart remarks, which weren't helping the situation. He told me that Dilley shouldn't be mollycoddled. From then on, I made sure I stood at mid-on and mid-off, where the ball could be returned to me and I could walk it over to Dilley and hopefully help him with a few constructive pieces of advice and some kind words. When we moved on to Guyana – having lost by an innings in Trinidad – I had a long sit down with Botham to ouline my concerns. After this, I wasn't selected to play for England during his time as captain.

The West Indies were undoubtedly the world's greatest team back then. Their pace attack and the batting of Viv Richards made them almost unbeatable, which added to the pressure on Botham. After he quit and was replaced by Brearley, I thought I might be picked for Headingley. After all, it was my 'home'. If anyone knew the atmospheric vagaries of the ground, and the condition of the pitch, then it had to be me. I also knew that Brearley both respected me, and thought he could rely on my bowling.

Having been with Yorkshire for so long, I always had set space in which to get changed at Headingley. When I arrived for the Test, Botham had taken the place alongside it. 'Welcome back,' he said, stretching out his hand 'it's great to see you again'. If he thought it was so great, I said to myself, then why hadn't he tried to persuade me to rejoin the side earlier in the season? I have to say that I felt rather uncomfortable with the situation. But, as a professional, I had to get on with it. Brearley was the polar opposite of Botham. Given his training as a psychologist, he instinctively knew – or soon worked out – who needed a kick in the backside or an arm wrapped around their shoulder to make them perform. He watched his players closely and his expertise meant he knew what to say to them too.

It seemed, however, that not even Brearley's extraordinary powers could guide us to a win this time. Half way through our second innings, Australia were already planning for a day off – and also believed the Ashes were almost theirs again. I remember sitting on the balcony with Dilley just before he went into bat. 'What should we do?' he asked. 'Just have a go,' I replied. He did. Dilley stood up and began bludgeoning boundaries. He hit the ball especially hard. At first, the Aussies didn't take much notice. After all, no one thought it would make any difference. It was dismissed as token resistance; something to make the scorecard look a little more respectable.

I'm convinced that Dilley's attitude and approach inspired Botham. At Somerset, he had a contest with Viv Richards to see which of them could strike the ball harder and furthest. He began to have the same contest with Dilley, and it became a fantastic piece of theatre. When Dilley was out, on for 56 off only 75 balls, I came in. On the way to the crease, I congratulated him on a magnificent innings. 'Just do the same,' he said. As I got to the middle, Botham came across. 'I suppose you're going to take a similar approach,' he said. The Australians were beginning to get frustrated rather than fearful, and I think I added to their sense of irritation because I'm a left-hander. The bowlers found themselves having to change their line from Botham to me and back again, and it disturbed them. There is always a 'tipping point' – the moment when the balance of a game shifts from one team to the other. And I noticed it when the Australians began to have more than one captain on the field. Kim Hughes was actually in charge, but soon Dennis Lillee, Geoff Lawson and Allan Border were waving fielders this way and that. Someone would be dispatched to the spot where the ball had just gone. The field became so spread that we could actually pick the gaps with our shots. My job was to persuade Botham not to try to hit every ball clean out of Headingley.

I made 29 off 31 deliveries before Lawson bowled me a slow-ish yorker, which I misjudged. It took my leg stump. I went back into the dressing room to be met by Brearley. 'How do you think we're going?' he asked. 'Well,' I said 'if we could get another fifty or sixty runs we might have a chance. But I don't really think so'. That conversation shows how much I knew!

Sometimes it can be difficult to chase small totals. I didn't expect it would be so difficult that the Aussies would fail to do it. On the evening before the final day, as expectations about our chances began to rise, I went into my local for a pint of Tetley's. 'I've put a fiver on England at 500-1,' someone told me. 'You can have twenty per-cent if you pull it off'. I'd experienced so much pressure that I didn't want to think about the Test, let alone talk about it. The money didn't interest me.

Even though my figures didn't suggest so – I finished with 0-91 - I thought I'd bowled well in the first innings. Watching the highlights of each day again fairly recently, I noticed that the edges I got simply hadn't carried – usually falling six inches short – and that there'd been a lot of playing and missing against me. The wickets had gone to Botham. He took six of them.

As the second innings began, I just had to put the ball on a length, or just short of one, and see what I could do. With the Australians only 56 for one, the match looked as good as over. At lunch, we pin-pointed Border as the dangerman. If we could get him out, we thought we'd got an outside chance.

I always enjoyed bowling to left-handers. I had the ability to make the ball come into them and I tried to keep my line tight. After the interval, I bowled the first over – and gave Border what I regard as three of the best balls I've ever delivered in Test cricket. The first rose and cut back so sharply that Bob Taylor had to dive down the leg side. The second landed around off stump, but came in before cutting away again like an off-break. Taylor was in front of first slip when he took it. The third was almost identical to the first. Border tried to leave it – but the ball didn't leave him. It caught the bottom of the bat and rattled into his stumps. It was the only wicket I claimed in the match. It is also the most pivotal one I've ever taken. I have the most wonderful photograph as a souvenir. The camera shutter clicks just as the ball is taking Border's off-stump.

While everyone talks about Botham's innings, the key to knocking over Australia at the end was Bob Willis. He didn't particularly like bowling down the hill at Headingley, which is where Brearley put him. Again, the captain was right. Willis was fierce, nasty and always challenging. He came at them like a rocket and finished with a fantastic 8-43. I'll never forget the shattered look on the faces of the Aussies – all out for 111 and beaten by 18 runs. The rest was just a blur: shouting, yelling, a packed dressing room, champagne, TV crews and reporters.

I arrived at my hotel in Sheffield to prepare for Yorkshire versus Sri Lanka at Abbeydale Park. That night I sat in bed with a bottle of champagne and two pints of Guinness. The following morning everything was rather hazy to say the least. But I got one more lucky break . . . it was pouring down and thankfully we didn't have to play. I doubt I'd have seen the ball.

I figured in other memorable Ashes moments. I saw first hand, and close up, the frightening speed of Dennis Lillee and Jeff Thomson on my first tour in 1974-75. When I got back to the nets at Yorkshire, John Hampshire admitted that he'd ducked against them while sitting on his sofa at home. I also played in the Centenary Tests of 1977 at Melbourne and 1980 at Lord's. In Melbourne, I pulled a hamstring on the first day and spent the rest of the match heavily strapped. I still bowled more overs than anyone else in the second innings – 27.6 of eight balls apiece – and took four wickets for match figures of 7-143. Whenever I left my hotel room, I ran into one of the all-time Greats. The atmosphere on the opening morning was tense not just because there were around 90,000 people in the MCG, but also because we all knew that anyone who'd ever played in an Ashes Test – from Donald Bradman to Ray Lindwall, from Denis Compton to Harold Larwood – was sitting in that crowd.

I still can't 'escape' Headingley '81, however. Every so often, my phone will ring and someone will still want to chat about the match, which was voted Britain's most memorable sporting moment. It'll still be talked about one hundred years from now.

There is an interesting postscript to the '81 series. In the next Test at Edgbaston, Botham came across to me and said: 'I don't know why I've come on to bowl – you're doing so much better than me'. I replied that I thought the captain knew what he was doing. Australia needed only 151 to win and were 105-5. Botham promptly took five wickets for one run in 28 balls and we won by 29 runs.

No captain other than Brearley could have done it.

Ian Botham leaves the Headingley pitch after England had beaten Australia in 1981 (YP)

SCORECARD

Result: England won by 18 runs

Toss: Australia, who chose to bat first

Series: 6-match series level 1-1

Player of the match: IT Botham (England)

Umpires: DGL Evans and BJ Meyer

Australia 1st innings		RUNS
J Dyson	b Dilley	102
GM Wood	lbw b Botham	34
TM Chappell	c Taylor b Willey	27
KJ Hughes	c & b Botham	89
RJ Bright	b Dilley	7
GN Yallop	c Taylor b Botham	58
AR Border	lbw b Botham	8
RW Marsh	b Botham	28
GF Lawson	c Taylor b Botham	13
DK Lillee	not out	3
TM Alderman	not out	0
Extras	(b 4, lb 13, w 3, nb 12)	32
Total	(9 wickets dec; 155.2 overs)	401

Bowling	O	M	R	W	Econ
RGD Willis	30	8	72	0	2.40
CM Old	43	14	91	0	2.11
GR Dilley	27	4	78	2	2.88
IT Botham	39.2	11	95	6	2.41
P Willey	13	2	31	1	2.38
G Boycott	3	2	2	0	0.66

Fall of wickets 1-55 (Wood), 2-149 (Chappell), 3-196 (Dyson), 4-220 (Bright), 5-332 (Hughes), 6-354 (Border), 7-357 (Yallop), 8-396 (Lawson), 9-401 (Marsh)

England 1st innings		RUNS
GA Gooch	lbw b Alderman	2
G Boycott	b Lawson	12
JM Brearley	c Marsh b Alderman	10
DI Gower	c Marsh b Lawson	24
MW Gatting	lbw b Lillee	15
P Willey	b Lawson	8
IT Botham	c Marsh b Lillee	50
RW Taylor	c Marsh b Lillee	5
GR Dilley	c & b Lillee	13
CM Old	c Border b Alderman	0
RGD Willis	not out	1
Extras	(b 6, lb 11, w 6, nb 11)	34
Total	(all out; 50.5 overs)	174

Bowling	O	M	R	W	Econ
DK Lillee	18.5	7	49	4	2.60
TM Alderman	19	4	59	3	3.10
GF Lawson	13	3	32	3	2.46

Fall of wickets 1-12 (Gooch), 2-40 (Brearley), 3-42 (Boycott), 4-84 (Gower), 5-87 (Gatting), 6-112 (Willey), 7-148 (Taylor), 8-166 (Botham), 9-167 (Old), 10-174 (Dilley)

England 2nd innings (following on)		RUNS
GA Gooch	c Alderman b Lillee	0
G Boycott	lbw b Alderman	46
JM Brearley	c Alderman b Lillee	14
DI Gower	c Border b Alderman	9
MW Gatting	lbw b Alderman	1
P Willey	c Dyson b Lillee	33
IT Botham	not out	149
RW Taylor	c Bright b Alderman	1
GR Dilley	b Alderman	56
CM Old	b Lawson	29
RGD Willis	c Border b Alderman	2
Extras	(b 5, lb 3, w 3, nb 5)	16
Total	(all out; 87.3 overs)	356

Bowling	O	M	R	W	Econ
DK Lillee	25	6	94	3	3.76
TM Alderman	35.3	6	135	6	3.80
GF Lawson	23	4	96	1	4.17
RJ Bright	4	0	15	0	3.75

Fall of wickets 1-0 (Gooch), 2-18 (Brearley), 3-37 (Gower), 4-41 (Gatting), 5-105 (Willey), 6-133 (Boycott), 7-135 (Taylor), 8-252 (Dilley), 9-319 (Old), 10-356 (Willis)

Australia 2nd innings (target: 130 runs)		RUNS
J Dyson	c Taylor b Willis	34
GM Wood	c Taylor b Botham	10
TM Chappell	c Taylor b Willis	8
KJ Hughes	c Botham b Willis	0
GN Yallop	c Gatting b Willis	0
AR Border	b Old	0
RW Marsh	c Dilley b Willis	4
RJ Bright	b Willis	19
GF Lawson	c Taylor b Willis	1
DK Lillee	c Gatting b Willis	17
TM Alderman	not out	0
Extras	(lb 3, w 1, nb 14)	18
Total	(all out; 36.1 overs)	111

Bowling	O	M	R	W	Econ
IT Botham	7	3	14	1	2.00
GR Dilley	2	0	11	0	5.50
RGD Willis	15.1	3	43	8	2.83
CM Old	9	1	21	1	2.33
P Willey	3	1	4	0	1.33

Fall of wickets 1-13 (Wood), 2-56 (Chappell), 3-58 (Hughes), 4-58 (Yallop), 5-65 (Border), 6-68 (Dyson), 7-74 (Marsh), 8-75 (Lawson), 9-110 (Lillee), 10-111 (Bright)

16

DARREN GOUGH

Born: September 18, 1970, Monk Bretton, Barnsley

As an inspirational all-rounder, who led with gusto and exuberance, he scored more than 4,600 first class runs (average 17.31) and took 855 wickets (average 27.15). In his 58 Tests, he was Man of Series against both West Indies and in Sri Lanka and played an integral role in England's four successive series wins between 2000 and 2001. Although injury deprived him of an Ashes tour and the World Cup, he returned in time for the summer of 2003, retiring from Test cricket after playing at Lord's against South Africa. He has another claim to fame. In 2005 he won the BBC's Strictly Come Dancing.

Test record:	
Span:	1972-81
Span	1994-2003
Matches:	58
Runs:	855
Highest score:	65
Average:	12.57
Wickets:	229
	(best 6-42)
Average:	28.39
Catches:	13

Melbourne:
December 26, 27, 28, 29, 1998

I know that this is going to sound extremely bizarre. But, even though I took a hat-trick against Australia in Sydney, it doesn't rank as the greatest moment of my Ashes career.

Of course, I'm extremely proud of the hat-trick, which is soaked in history. It was the first at Sydney since 1891-92. It was also the first by an Englishman in an Ashes Test since Jack Hearne in 1899. And, as you'd expect, the feat is extremely rare. In fact, only 11 bowlers have taken three wickets with consecutive balls for England. Apart from myself and Hearne, there's Billy Bates in 1883; Johnny Briggs in 1892; George Lohmann in 1896; Maurice Allom in 1930; Tom Goddard in 1938; Peter Loader in 1957; Dominic Cork in 1995; Matthew Hoggard in 2004 and Ryan Sidebottom in 2008.

Mine came on day one as we were trying to draw the series. The Australian captain Mark Taylor, who won all five tosses against Alec Stewart, predictably decided to bat and the Waugh brothers flayed us to all parts; Mark ended up with 121 and Steve with 96.

The real drama for me came right at the end of the final session. The hands of the clock were already well past six, and the Aussies were comfortable on 321-6. I hadn't bowled well earlier. I'd felt surprisingly lethargic, as if I need a break to recharge myself.

Local hero Darren Gough makes a hearty appeal for the LBW of Australia's Michael Slater. Headingley 2001. (PA)

When the new ball arrived, Alec didn't hand it over to me straight away. Instead he asked: 'Do you want a rest?' I shook my head. I thought I'd plough on, drag up some reserves of energy and try to let the occasional delivery rip.

With my fourth ball, Ian Healy got a thick edge to an outswinger. He took a step or two towards the pavilion, but suddenly stopped, as though a speck of dust had fallen in his eye. The umpire, Steve Dunne wasn't impressed with the gamesmanship. The finger went up . . .and Healy was on his way again.

Next in was Stuart MacGill. I tried to york him, and the ball came back and shattered his stumps.

The ironic thing is that I'd almost taken a hat-trick in the second Test at Perth. I'd removed Healy, trapping him lbw, and then Damien Fleming, who nudged a catch to Graeme Hick. The batsman who separated me from it – and another honourable mention in Wisden – was a rabbit: Colin 'Funky' Miller.

So I kept telling myself that old adage about forcing the batsman to play. I was thinking: 'Make sure you get the ball on target' this time. Miller lunged at a ball of full length and it left him in the air, clipping off-stump at the very last moment.

I was mobbed from all sides. Alex Tudor bit the back of my head by accident (yes, I know it seems ridiculous).

When I started celebrating, I thought my wife, my mum and dad and family were part of the 43,000 crowd. I didn't realise until later that, trying to beat the traffic, the Gough party had slipped away to Coogee, the coastal resort where all of them were staying. They didn't see my hat-trick at all, but heard it on the radio travelling back to the hotel.

Journalists asked me afterwards whether what I'd done was the pinnacle for me against Australia. When I shook my head, I'm sure there were some people in the room who didn't believe what I'd said or thought I was indulging in an extravagant leg pull.

But I spoke nothing but the truth. For the sweetest moment came in the previous Test at Melbourne, which we won by just 12 runs. Even now, I feel exactly the same.

Having lost at Perth and Adelaide, we were 2-0 down and Australia were treating the remaining matches like a royal procession before coronation day. We abruptly turned the series into a contest again. We made 270, and Australia replied with 340. Our second innings brought 244 – leaving the Aussies with what, on the face of it, looked a straightforward 175. The team was in its pomp too: Steve Waugh reached 7,000 Test runs, and Healy took his 350th catch in that match.

At the back of our minds, however, we believed the Aussies had a problem chasing small totals. Their focus began to get blurry and we could throw them off their stride. With the scoreboard showing them on 103-2, our logic – and our optimism – seemed hopelessly flawed.

Everything changed with a miracle catch from Mark Ramprakash, who took a meaty pull from Justin Langer with one hand off Alan Mullally. Langer thought he was seeing things.

Dean Headley promptly took four for four in just 13 balls.

I was sure Steve Waugh, who was still batting, would want to go off and finish the job in the morning. The session had lasted ten minutes short of four hours and it was nearly 7.30pm. But Waugh decided to say on the field. We needed three wickets. He needed just 14 runs.

I was on my knees. Dean and I had bowled 16 overs straight, and yet Alec wouldn't take either of us off. 'We can't risk it,' he said. 'A new bowler might let something loose go – and then it'd be over'.

Waugh made one fatal error. Dean claimed Matt Nicholson, getting him caught behind by Warren Hegg, which brought in MacGill. In the previous innings, when there'd been no pressure, Waugh allowed MacGill to take the strike on his way to a career best 43. With so much at stake, I never imagined that he'd do the same again. But I was wrong.

Waugh took a single off the opening ball of my 16th over, and I playfully asked him whether he was thinking about his average. I got a scowl in return.

I ran in hard, as though my life depended on it. The ball beat MacGill for pace and moved slightly. His stumps were splayed all over the place.

Waugh was now trapped at the non-striker's end, unable to preserve or protect the last batsmen, Glen McGrath, who would take his tally of Test ducks to 18 – an Aussie record – after the fifth Test. McGrath got through his first ball from me, but not the second. It struck him on the toes. It was plumb lbw.

I'd never celebrated so wildly before. And I never celebrated so wildly afterwards either. I thrust out my chest and put my arms against my side, as if I was auditioning for the Hollywood version of Tarzan. I also yanked out one of the stumps as a souvenir and lifted it over my head.

I'd never beaten Australia before in a Test. I went wild. All the pent up frustration and anguish I'd suffered, as one defeat had followed another, came out in a gush of invective. I dashed up to a TV cameraman and yelled: 'Shove that up your arse, you Aussie ******'. The problem was that the poor guy was working for Sky. My less than complimentary 'performance' was repeated for the next 24 hours.

The night was filled with drinking and singing – first Oasis' greatest hits and then the National Anthem. We were still at it two days later when we watched the New Year come in with fireworks over the Sydney Harbour Bridge. For the record, we lost the final Test by 98 runs.

I still think fondly about Melbourne because of the joy it brought.

I've had some wonderful moments touring Australia. Four years earlier, Graham Gooch and I had gone to visit Harold Larwood. He lived in a modest bungalow a few miles from the SCG. 'He won't talk about Bodyline,' we were told. Harold, bless him, talked about nothing else. He talked us through the 98 he'd got at Sydney in 1933 and how he'd hobbled off during England's second innings with Donald Bradman beside. He showed

Daren Gough celebrates the England victory at the 4th Test in Melbourne 1998 (Patrick Eagar)

us the ashtray which his beloved skipper Douglas Jardine had given him: 'To Harold for the Ashes' read the inscription.

And on the 1998-99 tour I was touched by the solidarity of the lads before the Test at Brisbane. My granddad Fred died the day before the opening day. I didn't ask whether I was permitted to wear a black arm band in his honour – I just did it and hang the consequences. But I was very emotional when Alec said as we took the field: 'If he wears it, we all wear it. When one of us is hurting, we stick by him'.

Everyone in the team wore a black armband.

I'd wanted to go home afterwards to pay my respects. My dad urged me to stay. 'It's what Fred would have wanted,' he said.

The advice was right. And because of it I claimed my hat-trick – and helped to beat the Aussies in a Test.

SCORECARD

Result: England won by 12 runs
Toss: Australia, who chose to field first
Series: Australia led the 5-match series 2-1
Test debuts: MJ Nicholson (Aus); WK Hegg (Eng)

Player of the match: DW Headley (England)
Umpires: SA Bucknor (West Indies) and DJ Harper
TV umpire: GTD Morrow
Match referee: JR Reid (New Zealand)

England 1st innings

		RUNS
MA Atherton	c Healy b McGrath	0
AJ Stewart	b MacGill	107
MA Butcher	c Langer b McGrath	0
N Hussain	c Healy b Nicholson	19
MR Ramprakash	c McGrath b SR Waugh	63
GA Hick	c Fleming b MacGill	39
WK Hegg	c Healy b SR Waugh	3
DW Headley	c Taylor b McGrath	14
D Gough	b MacGill	11
ARC Fraser	not out	0
AD Mullally	lbw b MacGill	0
Extras	(lb 7, w 1, nb 6)	14
Total	(all out; 76 overs)	270

Bowling	O	M	R	W	Econ
GD McGrath	22	5	64	3	2.90
DW Fleming	19	3	71	0	3.73
MJ Nicholson	10	0	59	1	5.90
SCG MacGill	19	2	61	4	3.21
SR Waugh	6	2	8	2	1.33

Fall of wickets 1-0 (Atherton, 0.5 ov), 2-4 (Butcher, 2.5 ov), 3-81 (Hussain, 22.5 ov), 4-200 (Stewart, 51.4 ov), 5-202 (Ramprakash, 52.5 ov), 6-206 (Hegg, 56.1 ov), 7-244 (Headley, 70.5 ov), 8-266 (Hick, 73.5 ov), 9-270 (Gough, 75.1 ov), 10-270 (Mullally, 75.6 ov)

Australia 1st innings

		RUNS
MA Taylor	c Hick b Gough	7
MJ Slater	lbw b Gough	1
JL Langer	c Hussain b Gough	44
ME Waugh	lbw b Fraser	36
SR Waugh	not out	122
DS Lehmann	c Hegg b Gough	13
IA Healy	c Headley b Fraser	36
DW Fleming	c Hick b Mullally	12
MJ Nicholson	b Gough	5
SCG MacGill	c Hegg b Mullally	43
GD McGrath	b Mullally	0
Extras	(b 4, lb 6, nb 11)	21
Total	(all out; 98.3 overs)	340

Bowling	O	M	R	W	Econ
D Gough	28	7	96	5	3.42
DW Headley	25	3	86	0	3.44
AD Mullally	21.3	5	64	3	2.97
MR Ramprakash	2	0	6	0	3.00
ARC Fraser	22	0	78	2	3.54

Fall of wickets 1-13 (Slater, 4.3 ov), 2-26 (Taylor, 10.1 ov), 3-98 (ME Waugh, 29.4 ov), 4-127 (Langer, 40.4 ov), 5-151 (Lehmann, 46.2 ov), 6-209 (Healy, 61.5 ov), 7-235 (Fleming, 71.3 ov), 8-252 (Nicholson, 76.6 ov), 9-340 (MacGill, 98.1 ov), 10-340 (McGrath, 98.3 ov)

England 2nd innings

		RUNS
MA Atherton	b Fleming	0
AJ Stewart	c Slater b MacGill	52
MA Butcher	c Slater b MacGill	14
DW Headley	b McGrath	1
N Hussain	c Slater b Nicholson	50
MR Ramprakash	b Nicholson	14
GA Hick	b Fleming	60
WK Hegg	c MacGill b Nicholson	9
D Gough	c Slater b MacGill	4
ARC Fraser	not out	7
AD Mullally	c & b McGrath	16
Extras	(b 2, lb 4, nb 11)	17
Total	(all out; 80.2 overs)	244

Bowling	O	M	R	W	Econ
GD McGrath	20.2	5	56	2	2.75
DW Fleming	17	4	45	2	2.64
MJ Nicholson	15	4	56	3	3.73
SCG MacGill	27	3	81	3	3.00
ME Waugh	1	1	0	0	0.00

Fall of wickets 1-5 (Atherton, 1.5 ov), 2-61 (Butcher, 17.5 ov), 3-66 (Headley, 24.1 ov), 4-78 (Stewart, 29.3 ov), 5-127 (Ramprakash, 46.2 ov), 6-178 (Hussain, 63.1 ov), 7-202 (Hegg, 69.6 ov), 8-221 (Gough, 74.2 ov), 9-221 (Hick, 75.1 ov), 10-244 (Mullally, 80.2 ov)

Australia 2nd innings (target: 175 runs)

		RUNS
MJ Slater	lbw b Headley	18
MA Taylor	c Headley b Mullally	19
JL Langer	c Ramprakash b Mullally	30
ME Waugh	c Hick b Headley	43
SR Waugh	not out	30
DS Lehmann	c Hegg b Headley	4
IA Healy	c Hick b Headley	0
DW Fleming	lbw b Headley	0
MJ Nicholson	c Hegg b Headley	9
SCG MacGill	b Gough	0
GD McGrath	lbw b Gough	0
Extras	(b 4, lb 1, nb 4)	9
Total	(all out; 46.4 overs)	162

Bowling	O	M	R	W	Econ
D Gough	15.4	2	54	2	3.44
DW Headley	17	5	60	6	3.52
AD Mullally	10	4	20	2	2.00
ARC Fraser	4	0	23	0	5.75

Fall of wickets 1-31 (Slater, 5.5 ov), 2-41 (Taylor, 10.5 ov), 3-103 (Langer, 26.5 ov), 4-130 (ME Waugh, 33.5 ov), 5-140 (Lehmann, 35.6 ov), 6-140 (Healy, 37.2 ov), 7-140 (Fleming, 37.5 ov), 8-161 (Nicholson, 45.5 ov), 9-162 (MacGill, 46.2 ov), 10-162 (McGrath, 46.4 ov)

Paul Jarvis in action against Australia at Edgbaston in 1989. (Patrick Eagar)

PAUL JARVIS

Born: June 29, 1965, Redcar

In 1981, at only 16 years and two months, he became the youngest player to represent Yorkshire. Six years later he finished his best season with 87 wickets and took 4-43 in the Benson and Hedges Cup final win over Northamptonshire. After leaving Yorkshire in 1993, he moved to Sussex and eventually finished his career at Somerset. He claimed 654 first class wickets at 28.92, made nine Test appearances and also played 16 One Day Internationals.

Test record:

Span:	1988-1993
Matches:	9
Wickets: 21 (best 4-107)	
Average:	45.95
Runs:	132
Highest score:	29 not out
Average:	10.15
Catches:	2

Lord's :
June 22, 23, 24, 26, 27, 1989

Even now, the summer of 1989 stirs conflicting emotions because it effectively pushed me into making a decision about the future direction of my career. It happened like this:

With an Ashes series looming, I logically expected to be in the team for the start of it. After all, I'd played in two Tests the previous summer against the West Indies, and there'd been no winter tour so no one else could stake a claim for my place. The selectors also chose me in the squad for the one-day Texaco Trophy matches against Australia before the Tests began. And the venue of the opening Test couldn't have been more perfect. It was Headingley – not only my own ground, but also a place where I performed well and consistently. I took a lot of wickets for Yorkshire there. But I didn't play in the one-day internationals, which meant I had a week off. When I returned from England duty, Yorkshire weren't playing either. It left me with another blank few days.

So, despite my knowledge of Headingley's conditions, and my track record of bowling on it, the England selectors ignored me. Although their reasoning was never properly explained to me, the gist seemed to be that I'd not bowled a sufficient number of overs to force my way in. Strangely enough, the other message was that England wanted a particular type of bowler. They'd made a 'horses for courses' decision. Derek Pringle, Phil

Newport and Neil Foster got the call instead. I was flabbergasted. So was my captain at Yorkshire, Phil Carrick. No other bowler knew the Headingley 'course' like me. Looking back, perhaps it was a lucky escape. Australia batted first, scored 601-7 declared and eventually won the match by 210 runs.

Having been overlooked for the Test in my own backyard, I didn't imagine I'd be called up for Lord's. Especially as Angus Fraser was pushing for his debut and he knew Lord's as well as I knew Headingley. Surely England would pick him? I'd always relished Lord's. I felt the same way about it as a footballer does about Wembley. It's more than just the obvious history and tradition of the place. You get a sense of it when you come down the stairs from the dressing rooms and walk through the Long Room before trotting down the concrete steps between the MCC members, and then feel your studs begin to bite into turf. The sense of anticipation and excitement hangs in the air. Naturally, there's a marked difference between the County circuit and a Test. But there's also a difference between a Test anywhere else, and a Test at Lord's. Even those people who normally don't watch cricket, or merely take a passing interest in it, seem to get hooked on the Lord's Test – and especially when the Ashes are at stake.

I'd usually played well there in the Championship against Middlesex, and I'd performed well in the 1987 Benson and Hedges Cup final when Yorkshire beat Northamptonshire and I finished with figures of 4-43. If the call did come against the Aussies, I thought I'd make a decent fist of it. The call did come – but, in truth, I tried too hard to prove the selectors had been wrong to leave me out at Headingley. I liked bowling from the pavilion end. I always attempted to dart the ball away from the right handed batsman. With the infamous Lord's ridge, I knew – especially with my skiddy action – that I could cause problems if I pitched on off stump and the ball held its line. I tended to catch batsmen on the crease. On the other hand, the Nursery End always felt alien to me, as if I was bowling against the grain. Guess where I bowled most of my overs?

Australia made 528 and I finished with the hardly inspiring figures of 1-150 (the 'one' was Ian Healy, who I had caught behind). As the Aussies didn't require much of a score to beat us, I only got through 9.2 overs in the second innings. I wasn't due to play at Edgbaston in the Third Test. I was pushed into the side at the last moment because Neil Foster injured his finger. My greatest contribution to the cause wasn't a wicket – though I claimed Geoff Marsh in the second innings – but 22 runs, which I scored as last man. We were fighting to avoid the follow-on. I decided to bat as normally as I could. If the ball was there to be hit, I made sure I made clean contact. I straight drove Geoff Lawson for four to ensure we didn't have to suffer the indignity of batting again. We eked out a draw, but I could sense that I wouldn't be figuring in the next Test. The captain, David Gower, preferred to bowl Graham Gooch rather than me. I bowled six overs in the second innings; he bowled 14.

My treatment bewildered me. Under Mike Gatting, I always felt included as part of the whole team. Under Gower, I hardly regarded myself as part of it at all. Gatting would bring me into discussions, and let you in on his thinking. He was good at trying to urge me on. Gower used to throw me the ball as though he'd decided it was 'my turn' rather than for any specific purpose. It's a shame. I used to watch and admire Gower as a player. As a captain, however, I found him too distant. Communication between the players and the

England selectors was also exceptionally poor. You never found out why you'd been dropped from a team. You never found out why you'd been picked either. You normally discovered your fate – good or bad – from Ceefax or the Press. I'd begun to think that there wasn't much going for me as far as England was concerned.

I'd just turned 24 and I was strong willed. I suffered back trouble now and again, which worried me at such a young age. I was also a married man with a young family and a big mortgage, who was earning £1,500 for each Test and £10,000 per summer from Yorkshire. If I didn't tour in the winter, I had to find part-time jobs to help pay the bills. I'd already been asked whether I wanted to tour South Africa, who were then still banned from Tests. When I weighed up my prospects, I decided to take the contract for a 'rebel' tour.

It might have been so different – if 1989 had been more rewarding with England.

SCORECARD

Result: Australia won by 6 wickets

Toss: England, who chose to bat first

Series: Australia led the 6-match series 2-0

Player of the match: SR Waugh (Australia)

Umpires: HD Bird and NT Plews

England 1st innings		RUNS
GA Gooch	c Healy b Waugh	60
BC Broad	lbw b Alderman	18
KJ Barnett	c Boon b Hughes	14
MW Gatting	c Boon b Hughes	0
DI Gower	b Lawson	57
RA Smith	c Hohns b Lawson	32
JE Emburey	b Alderman	0
RC Russell	not out	64
NA Foster	c Jones b Hughes	16
PW Jarvis	c Marsh b Hughes	6
GR Dilley	c Border b Alderman	7
Extras	(lb 9, nb 3)	12
Total	(all out; 86.5 overs)	286

Bowling	O	M	R	W	Econ
TM Alderman	20.5	4	60	3	2.88
GF Lawson	27	8	88	2	3.25
MG Hughes	23	6	71	4	3.08
SR Waugh	9	3	49	1	5.44
TV Hohns	7	3	9	0	1.28

Fall of wickets 1-31 (Broad), 2-52 (Barnett), 3-58 (Gatting), 4-131 (Gooch), 5-180 (Gower), 6-185 (Emburey), 7-191 (Smith), 8-237 (Foster), 9-253 (Jarvis), 10-286 (Dilley)

Australia 1st innings		RUNS
GR Marsh	c Russell b Dilley	3
MA Taylor	lbw b Foster	62
DC Boon	c Gooch b Dilley	94
AR Border	c Smith b Emburey	35
DM Jones	lbw b Foster	27
SR Waugh	not out	152
IA Healy	c Russell b Jarvis	3
MG Hughes	c Gooch b Foster	30
TV Hohns	b Emburey	21
GF Lawson	c Broad b Emburey	74
TM Alderman	lbw b Emburey	8
Extras	(lb 11, nb 8)	19
Total	(all out; 158 overs)	528

Bowling	O	M	R	W	Econ
GR Dilley	34	3	141	2	4.14
NA Foster	45	7	129	3	2.86
PW Jarvis	31	3	150	1	4.83
JE Emburey	42	12	88	4	2.09
GA Gooch	6	2	9	0	1.50

Fall of wickets 1-6 (Marsh), 2-151 (Taylor), 3-192 (Boon), 4-221 (Border), 5-235 (Jones), 6-265 (Healy), 7-331 (Hughes), 8-381 (Hohns), 9-511 (Lawson), 10-528 (Alderman)

England 2nd innings		RUNS
GA Gooch	lbw b Alderman	0
BC Broad	b Lawson	20
KJ Barnett	c Jones b Alderman	3
MW Gatting	lbw b Alderman	22
DI Gower	c Border b Hughes	106
RA Smith	b Alderman	96
RC Russell	c Boon b Lawson	29
JE Emburey	not out	36
NA Foster	lbw b Alderman	4
PW Jarvis	lbw b Alderman	5
GR Dilley	c Boon b Hughes	24
Extras	(b 6, lb 6, nb 2)	14
Total	(all out; 130 overs)	359

Bowling	O	M	R	W	Econ
TM Alderman	38	6	128	6	3.36
GF Lawson	39	10	99	2	2.53
MG Hughes	24	8	44	2	1.83
AR Border	9	3	23	0	2.55
TV Hohns	13	6	33	0	2.53
SR Waugh	7	2	20	0	2.85

Fall of wickets 1-0 (Gooch), 2-18 (Barnett), 3-28 (Broad), 4-84 (Gatting), 5-223 (Gower), 6-274 (Russell), 7-300 (Smith), 8-304 (Foster), 9-314 (Jarvis), 10-359 (Dilley)

Australia 2nd innings (target: 118 runs)		RUNS
GR Marsh	b Dilley	1
MA Taylor	c Gooch b Foster	27
DC Boon	not out	58
AR Border	c sub (RJ Sims) b Foster	1
DM Jones	c Russell b Foster	0
SR Waugh	not out	21
Extras	(b 3, lb 4, nb 4)	11
Total	(4 wickets; 40.2 overs)	119

Bowling	O	M	R	W	Econ
GR Dilley	10	2	27	1	2.70
NA Foster	18	3	39	3	2.16
JE Emburey	3	0	8	0	2.66
PW Jarvis	9.2	0	38	0	4.07

Fall of wickets 1-9 (Marsh), 2-51 (Taylor), 3-61 (Border), 4-67 (Jones)

Did not bat IA Healy, MG Hughes, TV Hohns, GF Lawson, TM Alderman

KEN TAYLOR

Born: August 21, 1935, Primrose Hill, Huddersfield

He spent his winter playing for Huddersfield Town, then in the First (Premier) Division, and his summer playing for Yorkshire. He trained at Huddersfield Art School and then at the Slade School of Fine Art in London. He made his Yorkshire debut at 17 and Huddersfield Town debut at 18. He became a crucial member of the Yorkshire side which won seven Championships from 1959 to 1968. In 313 first class appearances, he scored 13,053 runs with a highest score of 203 not out. His art, which includes some outstanding portraits of cricketers and footballers, continues to be admired and praised.

Test record:	
Test span:	1959-64
Matches	3
Runs	57
Highest Score	24
Catches	1

Headingley:
July 2, 3, 4, 6, 1964

To say I didn't expect to play in what turned out to be my one and only Test against Australia is a mild understatement. I greeted my eleventh hour call up with shock. I'd prepared myself for the far less onerous task of being 12th man, watching from the dressing room and fetching and carrying the drinks when duty demanded it.

Instead, early on the morning of the match, I was told I'd be taking the place of Colin Cowdrey, who abruptly declared himself unfit. Colin had a back problem. He'd batted twice against Cambridge University earlier in the week, making 70 in the second innings, before driving from Kent to Yorkshire. A combination of the long drive and a reasonably long innings exacerbated his condition.

When the chance to play in a Test arrives, you always want to grab it. But I was an opener in form who was suddenly put in to bat at number six. It is a different discipline, and I wasn't used to hanging around waiting to go in. As I sat in the dressing room, watching rather than batting, the nerves got to me. I was jittery and uncertain rather than confident and calm, which is no way to prepare for any innings, let alone one in a Test match.

As someone who played professional football as well as cricket, I think asking an opener to bat in the lower middle order is like asking a left-winger to switch to full back. To be

Ken Taylor with the tools of his trade. (YP)

successful, you need to have a different mental approach and a different set of skills to match it. I can't complain about not going in first. Our openers were Geoff Boycott (he'd made his debut at the beginning of the rubber) and John Edrich, who would establish themselves indisputably as the England's premier partnership during the rest of the 1960s and early 1970s. But batting so low down threw me out of my normal stride and style.

I scored 160 against the Aussies at Sheffield the previous month. It was the highest individual score against them by a Yorkshireman in a tour game. I eventually got to my century by moving from 85 to 99 in three balls – a six and two fours – before nudging the fourth for a single to reach the landmark. It must have impressed the selectors

But in the Headingley Test, I only made 14 in the first innings and nine in the second, being bowled by off spinner Tom Veivers. Or, in other words, I committed suicide. We made 268 in our first innings, which looked a decent score when Australia struggled to 178 for seven. And then Ted Dexter took the new ball. Peter Burge, on 38 not out, had been struggling against the flight and guile of Fred Titmus. Ted obviously thought Fred Trueman would rattle through the tail and leave us with a fairly healthy lead. The opposite was true. Fred did get Burge's wicket – but only after he'd heaped up 160 runs and taken the Aussies to 389.

We lost the match, which proved the only result. The other four were all drawn, though England were unlucky not have won the first two. Rain on the last day of both matches robbed them of victory.

I do have nice memories of the last day of the Trent Bridge match in spite of the rain. I was 12th man again and during the periods when we were rained off, I took my eight millimetre cine camera into the Australian dressing room. It was normal for players of both sides to wander into each other's dressing room for a chat. Some of the players were playing bridge and others reading or sleeping. Alec Bedser, Willie Watson, Denis Compton and a few more of the oldies were also there just wandering around. It was a lovely atmosphere and it was great to be there. I still have the cine film.

After Headingley, I didn't get to play for England again. The array of batting talent at the selectors' disposal was formidable. It made it difficult to break into the side. As well as Boycott and Edrich, there was Ken Barrington, Ted Dexter, Peter May, Brian Close, Tom Graveney, M J K Smith, Cowdrey and more.

There was a period much earlier in my career when Bryan Stott and I were so successful as an opening pair for Yorkshire (before Boycott came along) that England talked about putting us together in Tests. Brian Sellers, the Chairman of Cricket at Yorkshire, put a stop to it. He said we were too young. Who knows what would have happened if he'd kept his mouth shut.

Ex-players, especially of my vintage, are often asked about the differences between our era and modern day cricket. Cricket has changed considerably from a bowler's game to a batsman's game. In my day, after the start of a match, only the wicket ends were covered so the rain could not hinder the batsman's stance at the crease or the bowler's delivery stride. Because of these variable conditions, no side could take the field without two quick bowlers, two spinners and an all-rounder. Bats were much lighter, the spinners turned the ball more and the fast bowlers moved the ball off the seam because of the extra movement in the pitch. Batsmen had to be either nearer the ball to kill the spin or further away to play the ball later. Today wickets are covered at all times. The ball doesn't deviate off the line as much, so less movement by the batsmen is needed. They can play off the line of the ball with a 3lb-plus weighted bat and even an outside edge can go for six.

The game has changed and so has its spectators. Sledging, bad manners and aggression on the field finds its way on to the terraces. Umpires are continually being challenged by the bowlers – as referees are in football. Both cricket and football could take a leaf out of rugby league and union. A 'sin bin' – as in rugby – might be the answer.

On reflection, I don't think I was good enough – or had the right approach – to become a regular Test match player. I was always more than happy when the end of the season came – and I always looked forward to the football season starting. And vice-versa. I just don't know what I would have done if I had ever been selected to tour – though I was shortlisted four times. I enjoyed both games tremendously and, regardless of the money in cricket and football nowadays, I'm glad I played when I did.

One last thing. I did have one notable success against the Aussies. At the end of the tour game at Bramall Lane, the Milk Marketing Board organised a competition to see who had the longest throw.

It began early one evening. I managed to hurl the ball 112 yards and beat Paul Sheahan. My prize was £25. My wife Avril and I used it to take a long weekend break on the Northumberland coast. We paid for board, bed, petrol and food – including fish and chips at Seahouses – and still came home with £5 in our pockets.

How times change.

SCORECARD

Result: Australia won by 7 wickets

Toss: England, who chose to bat first

Series: Australia led the 5-match series 1-0

Test debut: RM Cowper (Australia)

Umpires: CS Elliott and WFF Price

England 1st innings		RUNS
G Boycott	c Simpson b Corling	38
JH Edrich	c Veivers b McKenzie	3
ER Dexter	c Grout b McKenzie	66
KF Barrington	b McKenzie	29
PH Parfitt	b Hawke	32
K Taylor	c Grout b Hawke	9
JM Parks	c Redpath b Hawke	68
FJ Titmus	c Burge b McKenzie	3
FS Trueman	c Cowper b Hawke	4
N Gifford	not out	1
JA Flavell	c Redpath b Hawke	5
Extras	(lb 9, nb 1)	10
Total	(all out; 103.3 overs)	268

Bowling	O	M	R	W	Econ
GD McKenzie	26	7	74	4	2.84
NJN Hawke	31.3	11	75	5	2.38
GE Corling	24	7	50	1	2.08
TR Veivers	17	3	35	0	2.05
RB Simpson	5	0	24	0	4.80

Fall of wickets 1-17 (Edrich), 2-74 (Boycott), 3-129 (Dexter), 4-138 (Barrington), 5-163 (Taylor), 6-215 (Parfitt), 7-232 (Titmus), 8-260 (Parks), 9-263 (Trueman), 10-268 (Flavell)

Australia 1st innings		RUNS
WM Lawry	run out	78
RB Simpson	b Gifford	24
IR Redpath	b Gifford	20
PJP Burge	c sub b Trueman	160
BC Booth	st Parks b Titmus	4
RM Cowper	b Trueman	2
TR Veivers	c Parks b Titmus	8
GD McKenzie	b Titmus	0
NJN Hawke	c Parfitt b Trueman	37
ATW Grout	lbw b Titmus	37
GE Corling	not out	2
Extras	(b 1, lb 8, w 2, nb 6)	17
Total	(all out; 158.3 overs)	389

Bowling	O	M	R	W	Econ
FS Trueman	24.3	2	98	3	4.00
JA Flavell	29	5	97	0	3.34
N Gifford	34	15	62	2	1.82
ER Dexter	19	5	40	0	2.10
FJ Titmus	50	24	69	4	1.38
K Taylor	2	0	6	0	3.00

Fall of wickets 1-50 (Simpson), 2-124 (Lawry), 3-129 (Redpath), 4-154 (Booth), 5-157 (Cowper), 6-178 (Veivers), 7-178 (McKenzie), 8-283 (Hawke), 9-372 (Grout), 10-389 (Burge)

England 2nd innings		RUNS
G Boycott	c Simpson b Corling	4
JH Edrich	c Grout b McKenzie	32
PH Parfitt	c Redpath b Hawke	6
KF Barrington	lbw b Veivers	85
ER Dexter	c Redpath b Veivers	17
JM Parks	c Booth b McKenzie	23
N Gifford	b McKenzie	1
K Taylor	b Veivers	15
FJ Titmus	c Cowper b Corling	14
FS Trueman	not out	12
JA Flavell	c Simpson b Corling	5
Extras	(b 6, lb 6, w 1, nb 2)	15
Total	(all out; 89.5 overs)	229

Bowling	O	M	R	W	Econ
GD McKenzie	28	8	53	3	1.89
NJN Hawke	13	1	28	1	2.15
GE Corling	17.5	6	52	3	2.91
TR Veivers	30	12	70	3	2.33
RB Simpson	1	0	11	0	11.00

Fall of wickets 1-13 (Boycott), 1-13* (Parfitt, retired not out), 2-88 (Edrich), 3-145 (Dexter), 4-156 (Barrington), 5-169 (Gifford), 6-184 (Parks), 7-192 (Taylor), 8-199 (Parfitt), 9-212 (Titmus), 10-229 (Flavell)

Australia 2nd innings (target: 109 runs)		RUNS
WM Lawry	c Gifford b Trueman	1
RB Simpson	c Barrington b Titmus	30
IR Redpath	not out	58
PJP Burge	b Titmus	8
BC Booth	not out	12
Extras	(b 1, lb 1)	2
Total	(3 wickets; 57 overs)	111

Bowling	O	M	R	W	Econ
FS Trueman	7	0	28	1	4.00
N Gifford	20	5	47	0	2.35
ER Dexter	3	0	9	0	3.00
FJ Titmus	27	19	25	2	0.92

Fall of wickets 1-3 (Lawry), 2-45 (Simpson), 3-64 (Burge)

Did not bat RM Cowper, TR Veivers, GD McKenzie, NJN Hawke, ATW Grout, GE Corling

33

Brian Close. (YP)

BRIAN CLOSE

Born: February 24, 1931, Rawdon, Leeds

The word most associated with him is courage. Not only did he withstand the bouncers of the West Indies in 1976 – most of which he absorbed on his 45 year-old body – but he was also a quite fearless short leg, once imperturbably statuesque when Garry Sobers went for a full blooded and fierce pull. When Sobers (rare for him) mistimed his shot, the catch was taken without an eye blink. He made nearly 35,000 first class runs, claimed 1,171 wickets and 813 catches. In 1949, he became the youngest player ever to play for England – aged 18 – against New Zealand. He captained Yorkshire, Somerset and England.

Test record:	
Span:	1949-1976
Matches:	22
Highest score:	70
Average:	25.34
Wickets:	18 (best 4-35)
Average:	29.55
Catches:	24

Melbourne:
December 22, 23, 26, 27, 1950

I was just 19 years old when I set sail for Australia with Freddie Brown's team in the autumn of 1950. I was naïve and unworldly. I'd never been abroad before, and I didn't drink or smoke.

I'd never seen an ocean-going liner, let alone climbed aboard one, and I spent the first day of our long journey exploring every part of it. But I was off on what I thought would be an awfully big adventure and my travelling companions were heroes of mine, such as Denis Compton, Cyril Washbrook and, of course, Len Hutton.

What followed were six of the most miserable months of my life. And because of it I came back as a tougher and more mature figure. In the adversity, and often abject misery of Australia, I grew up.

During my first summer with Yorkshire in 1949, I finished with the prized double: 1,098 runs and 113 wickets. Mid-way through it, I found myself picked unexpectedly – at just 18 years and 149 days – for England against New Zealand at Old Trafford. I was down to bat at number seven but Freddie Brown held me back in the order because quick runs were needed and there were only Les Jackson and Eric Hollies left when I did get in. Freddie said: 'Have a look at a couple and then give it a go.' I pushed a couple from Tom

Burtt, their slow left armer, back up the pitch and then, going for the big hit, was caught on the long on boundary and they were proper boundaries then not the shortened ones we have now in Test cricket. So I made a duck, and bowled 42 overs in two innings for 85 runs and the solitary wicket of Merv Wallace. The match finished tamely as a draw, and I went back to the County Championship.

I was lucky because I shouldn't have been playing at all. I ought to have been square bashing as part of my National Service, but when I went for my medical I had a soccer injury to my right knee and the MO said 'we don't want you going in and reporting sick as soon as you get there so we'll defer your call up'.

If it had not been deferred I would have been in the army and I would not have had the opportunity of playing for Yorkshire and might never have got the chance in the future, given the talent that was around. Yorkshire were doing so well that summer and there was news that I was going to be called up mid-season so my local MP, Maurice Webb, managed to get me a deferment until the end of the summer.

With the season over, I ended up going straight into the Army and faced up to the fact that my cricketing life was effectively on hold for a couple of years. In 1950, the only matches I played were for the Army and Combined Services and only the latter counted as first class. That's why it was a shock when I was selected for the Australian tour. I hadn't even scored a first class century. But Freddie Brown, the captain, wanted to blood someone young and give them a taste of Test cricket for the future.

I thought – wrongly, as it turned out – that I'd be guided and schooled as the junior member of the team. I thought – again wrongly – that I'd be given advice about what it was like to play in Australian conditions and that I'd hear some wise words about how to improve my technique. I wanted to find out more about playing specific shots, field-placings and the skills required in building a long innings. I waited for the senior amateurs and pros to draw me to one side and share their secrets about the game. I couldn't go and ask. Believe it or not, I was too shy. I didn't know how to approach them. But no one helped me. Not one of the seniors told me anything. When I needed someone to put an arm around my shoulder and tell me what to do and how to behave, it wasn't there and I'm afraid I didn't understand what was going on. I did later when I realised that the greats of that team had lost five years of their playing lives because of the war and didn't want to be bothered with a youngster when there was so much socialising to enjoy on a trip like that.

At the beginning of the tour, I made 108 not out against Western Australia. Another 105 not out came in the game with New South Wales Country Districts at Canberra. But my second century came at a high price. I tore the roots of a tendon in my groin during the innings and missed the first Test where we lost by 70 runs at Brisbane in what Jack Fingleton described as 'surely the craziest and maddest Test match of all time . . . certainly without counterpart in living memory'. The match was over in four days after rain so hard and intense that at one stage the entire ground was nearly washed away. The conditions became unplayable for batsmen. On the third day 20 wickets fell for a mere 130 runs. The so called 'mystery spinner' Jack Iverson, took four for 43 on his debut.

As the second Test approached at Melbourne Freddie Brown asked me about my fitness because, he said, being an all rounder my presence would balance the side. I told him the injury wasn't healed but if it was important I would play with it strapped up. I thought I'd be fine. During fielding practice, however, I went to take a catch, twisted awkwardly and felt the groin go again.

'How bad is it?' Brown asked me. 'I think it's only slight,' I replied, 'I'll be alright if I have it strapped'. It was an answer that I came to bitterly regret. You can't go into the Tests with half-fit players; certainly not against Australia. But I was young, keen to impress and unaware of the problems I might cause both for myself, the team and for Brown. I honestly thought my enthusiasm would get me through the match.

By the time, I got to bat we were already 54 for four, there were four balls to go before lunch and Iverson was bowling. I'd played against him in the state game at Melbourne and could 'read' him. His natural ball was a googly and the leg spinner the rarity so when he bowled one down the leg side I went to sweep but didn't take into account the extra bounce of Aussie pitches and got a top edge to Sam Loxton at backward square leg. I'll always remember walking back to the dressing room and the funeral-like silence in the place. I spent lunch almost in tears. Australia won the Test by 28 runs. More than a quarter of a century later, during the 1977 Centenary Test in Melbourne, the Australian Ian Johnson, who played in that match, told me that he'd noticed my glum face and said to Brown: 'He's a bit down. Why don't you go and speak to him'. Brown apparently replied: 'Let the ****** stew. He deserves it'. I actually caught Ian on the boundary in the second innings. My injury was so bad I could barely run by then.

A few days later I was in such a bad way that Brown arranged for me to visit a specialist in Hobart before the match with Tasmania. Fortunately for me, the consultant had seen a similar injury before. 'You've ruptured the roots of a tendon,' he said. 'You won't be fit to play for at least a month'. Denis Compton was stand-in skipper because Brown, Len Hutton and a few other of the seniors, were taking a break on the mainland. I gave him the specialist's report, he read it and promptly tore it in half and threw the pieces on the floor. 'I couldn't care less what the doctor says,' he said 'You're playing in the match at Launceston'. I had no option but to carry on. Back in mainland Australia I was told to play against the Victoria Country X1 at Geelong where the tendon snapped completely. In those days I was bowling fast and had taken a wicket early on but in the fourth over I fell in an untidy heap and had to be carried off the field. I was laid on a table and for the rest of the day I was sick and feverish. Ice packs had to be brought for my head. The senior players who knew little about the history of the injury just cursed me for, as they thought, letting the side down and I took no further part in the tour.

I finished the tour with a miserable batting average of 23.10, and I took only four wickets at 61.50. But I don't know what I'd have done without Bill Bowes, the former Yorkshire and England fast bowler. He was working as a journalist, and did his utmost to make me feel wanted and at home. He was almost the only person to whom to turn when I felt down – and that happened often because up until then I'd done little but play sport and not being able to participate was hugely depressing. Bill's attitude was in stark contrast to Brown's, which was: 'If the captain tells you to play with a broken leg, you do so – no arguments'.

Looking back on it, I think the interruption of National Service was significant. If I'd been able to play county cricket in 1950, building myself up physically and getting used to being alongside tough pros, I'd have been better equipped for an Australian tour both in an emotional and cricketing sense. However, the experience of that tour did me the world of good and the following summer I got a lot of runs for the Combined Services (including a ton against South Africa) and was the first to complete the double of 1,000 runs and 100 wickets in 1952, the second time for me and I still wasn't 21 years old!

I didn't play for England again for five years, and another six went by before I had the chance to face Australia. It turned into another bad experience because we lost a match at Old Trafford that we ought to have won – or, at the very least, drawn and I got the blame for it. We bowled out Australia for 190 and replied with 367 (I got 33 of them before getting a bad leg before decision when I edged into my pads), we were on top and should have stayed there. But we let their tail-enders Alan Davidson and Garth MacKenzie score too heavily. Davidson made 77 not out and MacKenzie scored 32 in a final stand of 98, which took the total to 432. It left us to score at almost 70 per hour to win the Test.

We replied well and sensibly; at one stage getting on for 150 with only one wicket down and on course. But then Richie Benaud went to bowl round the wicket and aimed for the rough created by fast bowler's follow through outside the left hander's off stump to make it harder to score but almost immediately he had Ted Dexter caught behind. Richie didn't spin the ball much during his career, but he was an exceptionally fine bowler – his line and length were immaculate. The ironic thing is that he came on to tie us down, and yet ended up with figures of six for 70 to win the match. When he went round the wicket I was sitting in the pavilion alongside Peter May, ready to bat at five. I remarked to the captain: 'For heaven's sake don't get two left handers in together otherwise the runs will dry up'. I'm afraid May took no notice.

After he was bowled round his legs and I went in, there was still a chance that we might beat the Aussies. We were only three down for 150. I had to be aggressive and push on as much as possible if we were going to win. Subba Row was playing carefully and even played out a maiden from Ken Mackay, a medium pace trundler, so it was up to me. I hit Richie for six over long on but then he pitched it further outside my off stump which made orthodox shots nigh on impossible. I tried to lap him out of the rough, the only scoring shot that was going to bear fruit and I thought I'd cleared Norman O'Neill, who was saving one just behind square leg. I can see the shot now. The ball is in the air, and I'm sure it's going over Norm's head then at the last moment, he leaps up and catches it with the first two fingers of his right hand. With another five wickets left, we should have shut up shop and settled for the draw. With runs not important Richie would have had to come back over the wicket and been easy to play because, apart from the follow throughs, it was still a good pitch. Unfortunately there was no policy, no instructions, we kept attacking and gave them the match. Even Fred Trueman went for a big hay-maker and was out to a simple catch. Guess who got the blame for being reckless? There was nothing said about others who threw their wickets away like Peter May, bowled round his legs sweeping, just an outcry about my choice of shot. I was described as irresponsible and Norman Yardley said on the radio that I shouldn't play for England again, let alone ever captain them.

I'm proud to say that I did captain my country, winning six of my seven Tests in charge and drawing the other. A lot of what I did when I became a skipper – of England, Yorkshire and Somerset – was the result of lessons learned in Australia in 1950-51. I always tried to help youngsters and bring them on. I knew that there were times when you needed to praise or criticise and help them improve their game and thinking. It's the one important positive that I took from my only tour Down Under.

My other experience of the Australians on the international stage came in 1972, five years after I'd been sacked, when I was called up to lead England in the one-day series against a side which included the Chappell brothers, Dennis Lillee, Jeff Thomson and Bob Massie, the swing bowler who took 16 wickets in the Lord's Test that season. I'm happy to say that I led England to a 2-1 series win and also had the great pleasure of captaining Somerset when we beat them at Bath.

SCORECARD

Result: Australia won by 28 runs

Toss: Australia, who chose to bat first

Series: Australia led the 5-match series 2-0

Test debut: KA Archer (Australia)

Umpires: GS Cooper and RJJ Wright

Australia 1st innings		RUNS
KA Archer	c Bedser b Bailey	26
AR Morris	c Hutton b Bedser	2
RN Harvey	c Evans b Bedser	42
KR Miller	lbw b Brown	18
AL Hassett	b Bailey	52
SJE Loxton	c Evans b Close	32
RR Lindwall	lbw b Bailey	8
D Tallon	not out	7
IWG Johnson	c Parkhouse b Bedser	0
WA Johnston	c Hutton b Bedser	0
JB Iverson	b Bailey	1
Extras	(b 4, lb 2)	6
Total	(all out; 59.1 overs)	194

Bowling	O	M	R	W	Econ
TE Bailey	17.1	5	40	4	1.75
AV Bedser	19	3	37	4	1.46
DVP Wright	8	0	63	0	5.90
FR Brown	9	0	28	1	2.33
DB Close	6	1	20	1	2.50

Fall of wickets 1-6 (Morris), 2-67 (Harvey), 3-89 (Archer), 4-93 (Miller), 5-177 (Loxton), 6-177 (Hassett), 7-192 (Lindwall), 8-193 (Johnson), 9-193 (Johnston), 10-194 (Iverson)

England 1st innings		RUNS
RT Simpson	c Johnson b Miller	4
C Washbrook	lbw b Lindwall	21
JG Dewes	c Miller b Johnston	8
L Hutton	c Tallon b Iverson	12
WGA Parkhouse	c Hassett b Miller	9
DB Close	c Loxton b Iverson	0
FR Brown	c Johnson b Iverson	62
TE Bailey	b Lindwall	12
TG Evans	c Johnson b Iverson	49
AV Bedser	not out	4
DVP Wright	lbw b Johnston	2
Extras	(b 8, lb 6)	14
Total	(all out; 62 overs)	197

Bowling	O	M	R	W	Econ
RR Lindwall	13	2	46	2	2.65
KR Miller	13	0	39	2	2.25
WA Johnston	9	1	28	2	2.33
JB Iverson	18	3	37	4	1.54
IWG Johnson	5	1	19	0	2.85
SJE Loxton	4	1	14	0	2.62

Fall of wickets 1-11 (Simpson), 2-33 (Dewes), 3-37 (Washbrook), 4-54 (Hutton), 5-54 (Close), 6-61 (Parkhouse), 7-126 (Bailey), 8-153 (Brown), 9-194 (Evans), 10-197 (Wright)

Australia 2nd innings		RUNS
KA Archer	c Bailey b Bedser	46
AR Morris	lbw b Wright	18
RN Harvey	run out	31
KR Miller	b Bailey	14
AL Hassett	c Bailey b Brown	19
SJE Loxton	c Evans b Brown	2
RR Lindwall	c Evans b Brown	7
D Tallon	lbw b Brown	0
IWG Johnson	c Close b Bedser	23
WA Johnston	b Bailey	6
JB Iverson	not out	0
Extras	(b 10, lb 5)	15
Total	(all out; 53.3 overs)	181

Bowling	O	M	R	W	Econ
TE Bailey	15	3	47	2	2.35
AV Bedser	16.3	2	43	2	1.96
DVP Wright	9	0	42	1	3.50
FR Brown	12	2	26	4	1.62
DB Close	1	0	8	0	6.00

Fall of wickets 1-43 (Morris), 2-99 (Archer), 3-100 (Harvey), 4-126 (Miller), 5-131 (Loxton), 6-151 (Lindwall), 7-151 (Tallon), 8-156 (Hassett), 9-181 (Johnson), 10-181 (Johnston)

England 2nd innings (target: 179 runs)		RUNS
RT Simpson	b Lindwall	23
C Washbrook	b Iverson	8
TE Bailey	b Johnson	0
L Hutton	c Lindwall b Johnston	40
JG Dewes	c Harvey b Iverson	5
WGA Parkhouse	lbw b Johnston	28
DB Close	lbw b Johnston	1
FR Brown	b Lindwall	8
TG Evans	b Lindwall	2
AV Bedser	not out	14
DVP Wright	lbw b Johnston	2
Extras	(b 17, lb 2)	19
Total	(all out; 63.7 overs)	150

Bowling	O	M	R	W	Econ
RR Lindwall	12	1	29	3	1.81
KR Miller	5	2	16	0	2.40
WA Johnston	13.7	1	26	4	1.40
JB Iverson	20	4	36	2	1.35
IWG Johnson	13	3	24	1	1.38

Fall of wickets 1-21 (Washbrook), 2-22 (Bailey), 3-52 (Simpson), 4-82 (Dewes), 5-92 (Hutton), 6-95 (Close), 7-122 (Brown), 8-124 (Evans), 9-134 (Parkhouse), 10-150 (Wright)

PHIL SHARPE

Born: Shipley, December 27, 1936

A quite exceptional slip fielder, who took 618 first class catches and 17 in his 12 Tests. He scored more than 22,500 first class runs (highest score 228) and finished with a Test average of 46.23. He retired in 1976.

Test record:	
Span:	1963-1969
Matches:	12
Runs:	786
Highest score:	111
Average:	46.23
Catches:	17

Trent Bridge:
June 4, 5, 6, 8, 9, 1964

When I was young, my father taught me about the importance of being a good fielder. 'If two batsmen are equal,' he said 'the place in the team will always go to the man who takes catches or stop runs'. Anyone who watches highlights of matches from the 1950s and 1960s – before one-day cricket really began to take hold – will probably be wondering what I'm talking about. The fielding in that era looks positively pedestrian compared to today's leaping and diving (some of it, in my opinion, unnecessary).

But my father was right. I even made my Test debut against the West Indies in 1963 purely on the basis of my ability in the slips. Charlie Griffith broke a bone in Colin Cowdrey's wrist in the previous, much talked about match at Lord's. Cowdrey came back into bat with his forearm in plaster and batted heroically to hold out for a tense and famous draw. Cowdrey was also excellent in the slips. Without him, England needed someone to fill the gap at Edgbaston - and I was called up as a result. I also had the bonus of making 85 not out.

I made my reputation as a slip fielder. In fact, I practised my fielding more than I did my batting. In those days we used the old fashioned, wooden slip cradle, but the ball came off at fairly predictable angles. We eventually draped a three-foot high curtain in front of

Phil Sharpe. (YP)

it so we couldn't see where the ball landed and consequently weren't able to work out in which direction it would fly. It was only later that we adopted the modern method in which someone uses the bat to deliberately steer or edge the ball towards us, which is far more realistic. But no amount of preparation made life easier for me when I eventually played my first Ashes Test at Trent Bridge in 1964. In fact, I dropped two catches.

With Yorkshire, I was used to giving our wicketkeeper Jimmy Binks plenty of room. With England, I didn't realise that Jim Parks wasn't too agile. Put it this way: he didn't dive much. When Bill Lawrie nicked one, I thought it was Parksy's. He didn't go for it and so I went late. I ended up pushing it 'round the post'. I was relieved when Bill only made 11 runs. But that wasn't the end of my troubles. I dropped Bobby Simpson – the Australian captain - straight in (and out) off Len Coldwell. He went on to make a half century – and I didn't catch anything during the entire Test. It really wasn't my match at all. Prince Philip arrived at Trent Bridge for the day. We were introduced to him in the players' dining room because it was teeming down outside. As captain, Ted Dexter accompanied the Prince along the line. When Ted eventually came to me, I could see his mind go blank. Eventually he turned to the Prince and said: 'This is Toby'. I instantly said: 'Actually it is Philip'. I think the Prince was rather confused. Toby was one of the nicknames given to me by a certain F S Trueman. He used to say that I looked like a Toby Jug when I stood in the slips. I didn't fare any better on the field at Lord's in the next Test. I only batted once – the match was affected by rain – and made 35. I hadn't done enough to retain my place. A player usually got two Tests at most to stake his claim, and I'd not done sufficiently well. Competition for a slot in the top order was particularly intense. There was always someone – usually of a very high calibre – waiting in the wings if you failed.

I nearly played against the Aussies again four years later. Yorkshire were about to bat against Essex at Southend. I was taking guard when the loudspeaker boomed: 'Will you stop the game please? Phil Sharpe is required at Headingley tomorrow for the Test match'. Tom Graveney was doubtful and I found myself ushered in as back up. As it turned out, Tom was fit enough not only to play but to captain the side. Colin Cowdrey withdrew with an injury, and yours truly spent two days as 12th man. By an odd twist of fate, Barry Jarman skippered the Australians because Lawry was also unfit. It suddenly became a popular quiz question: 'Who were the captains in the 1968 Headingley Test?' In Yorkshire circles, the match became known as Keith Fletcher's. Keith was first slip and dropped a couple of catches. The story is important because part of the skill of fielding is to know your wicket keepers (as I found out with Jim Parks) When he played with Essex, Keith stood next to Brian Taylor, who took the ball 'on the up'. It meant first slip had to stand four to five feet behind him to the quick bowlers. But Alan Knott took the ball 'on the drop', which meant that first slip had to stand only a foot or so behind him. This was Keith's problem at Headingley. He stood too far back, thereby widening the angle. He put down a couple of diving catches off John Snow (to be fair both would have been top class if he'd made them). If he'd been standing in the right place, he wouldn't have been obliged to dive at all. To add insult to injury, of course, he got fearful stick from the Yorkshire crowd because everybody thought he was playing instead of me. It wasn't the case; he was always going to play.

I'm often asked if I'd prefer to be playing now rather than back then. My answer is always the same. Not on your life. Not even, in fact, for all the money today's players earn. You see, we had a great social life. When I came into the Yorkshire side, I always remember Brian Sellers, the Chairman of Cricket at the time, telling me: 'If you are going to play this game, what you need is to get some ale down'. There was always beer available at lunchtime. In the early 60s, Yorkshire used to play Australia twice: once at Sheffield and again at Bradford Park Avenue. The '64 tourists were a great bunch. So much so that we invited three of them to go to a clay pigeon shoot on the Sunday of the Sheffield game (things were very civilised in those days). I was a member of a nomadic club called 'The Flakers', so called because one of the founder members, a rugby player, would have a habit of flaking out after the game each Saturday. His name was Geoff Lister and he eventually became my best man There were about 24 of us, and we'd take on anybody at anything: soccer, rugby union, cricket, hockey, table tennis – you name it. From the Australian party, Rex Sellers, Graham McKenzie and Tom Veivers joined us for the shoot and then afterwards we retreated to a suitable hostelry in Hathersage for a lunchtime session. I can't see it happening now.

SCORECARD

Result: Match drawn

Toss: England, who chose to bat first

Series: 5-match series level 0-0

Test debuts: GE Corling (Australia);
G Boycott (England)

Umpires: JS Buller and CS Elliott

England 1st innings		RUNS
G Boycott	c Simpson b Corling	48
FJ Titmus	c Redpath b Hawke	16
ER Dexter	c Grout b Hawke	9
MC Cowdrey	b Hawke	32
KF Barrington	c Lawry b Veivers	22
PJ Sharpe	not out	35
JM Parks	c Booth b Veivers	15
FS Trueman	c Simpson b Veivers	0
DA Allen	c Grout b McKenzie	21
LJ Coldwell	not out	0
Extras	(b 5, lb 11, nb 2)	18
Total	(8 wickets dec; 102 overs)	216

Did not bat JA Flavell

Bowling	O	M	R	W	Econ
GD McKenzie	28	7	53	1	1.89
GE Corling	23	7	38	1	1.65
NJN Hawke	35	15	68	3	1.94
TR Veivers	16	2	39	3	2.43

Fall of wickets 1-38 (Titmus), 2-70 (Dexter), 3-90 (Boycott), 4-135 (Barrington), 5-141 (Cowdrey), 6-164 (Parks), 7-165 (Trueman), 8-212 (Allen)

Australia 1st innings		RUNS
WM Lawry	c Barrington b Coldwell	11
IR Redpath	b Trueman	6
NC O'Neill	b Allen	26
PJP Burge	lbw b Trueman	31
BC Booth	run out	0
RB Simpson	c Barrington b Titmus	50
TR Veivers	c Trueman b Flavell	8
GD McKenzie	c Parks b Coldwell	4
NJN Hawke	not out	10
ATW Grout	c Parks b Coldwell	13
GE Corling	b Trueman	3
Extras	(lb 1, nb 5)	6
Total	(all out; 78.3 overs)	168

Bowling	O	M	R	W	Econ
FS Trueman	20.3	3	58	3	2.82
LJ Coldwell	22	3	48	3	2.18
DA Allen	16	8	22	1	1.37
JA Flavell	16	3	28	1	1.75
FJ Titmus	4	1	6	1	1.50

Fall of wickets 1-8 (Redpath), 2-37 (Lawry), 3-57 (O'Neill), 4-61 (Booth), 5-91 (Burge), 6-118 (Veivers), 7-137 (McKenzie), 8-141 (Simpson), 9-165 (Grout), 10-168 (Corling)

England 2nd innings		RUNS
ER Dexter	c O'Neill b McKenzie	68
FJ Titmus	lbw b McKenzie	17
MC Cowdrey	b McKenzie	33
KF Barrington	lbw b Corling	33
JM Parks	c Hawke b Veivers	19
PJ Sharpe	c & b Veivers	1
FS Trueman	c Grout b McKenzie	4
DA Allen	lbw b McKenzie	3
JA Flavell	c Booth b Corling	7
LJ Coldwell	not out	0
Extras	(b 2, lb 2, w 1, nb 3)	8
Total	(9 wickets dec; 66.5 overs)	193

Did not bat G Boycott

Bowling	O	M	R	W	Econ
GD McKenzie	24	5	53	5	2.20
GE Corling	15.5	4	54	2	3.41
NJN Hawke	19	5	53	0	2.78
TR Veivers	8	0	25	2	3.12

Fall of wickets 1-90 (Dexter), 2-95 (Titmus), 3-147 (Barrington), 4-174 (Parks), 5-179 (Sharpe), 6-180 (Cowdrey), 7-186 (Allen), 8-187 (Trueman), 9-193 (Flavell)

Australia 2nd innings (target: 242 runs)		RUNS
WM Lawry	run out	3
IR Redpath	c Parks b Flavell	2
NC O'Neill	retired hurt	24
PJP Burge	not out	4
BC Booth	not out	6
Extras	(nb 1)	1
Total	(2 wickets; 9.2 overs)	40

Did not bat RB Simpson, TR Veivers, GD McKenzie, NJN Hawke, ATW Grout, GE Corling

Bowling	O	M	R	W	Econ
FS Trueman	5	0	28	0	5.60
JA Flavell	4.2	0	11	1	2.53

Fall of wickets 1-3 (Lawry), 2-25 (Redpath), 2-31* (O'Neill, retired not out)

45

Bill Athey batting in Sydney, 1987.
(Patrick Eagar)

BILL ATHEY

Born: September 27, 1957, Middlesbrough

He scored 25,453 runs for three counties – Gloucestershire, Sussex and Yorkshire (he also appeared for Worcestershire in one-day cricket) – and finished with an average of 35.69. As well as Tests, he made 31 one-day appearances for England, including the World Cup final defeat against Australia in 1987. He also took 48 first class wickets.

Test record:	
Span:	1980-1988
Matches:	23
Runs:	919
Highest score:	123
Average:	22.97
100s:	1
Catches:	13

Brisbane:
November 14, 15, 16, 18, 19, 1986

There were supposedly only three things wrong with the 1986-87 tour party. We were the team who couldn't bat, couldn't bowl and couldn't field. We were also the team that Australia expected to roll over in front of a typically partisan home crowd. And, finally, we were the team who weren't given much of a chance by the bookmakers: one of them priced us at 4-1 against to retain the Ashes before we stepped on the plane.

The phrase about not being able to bat, bowl of field, which was coined by a journalist with his tongue pressed firmly in his cheek, really stuck with us throughout the 1986-87 series – first as condemnation of some indifferent performances in our warm-up matches and then as satire. We even had T-shirts printed with 'Can't bat, Can't bowl, Can't field' emblazoned across the front of them.

Of course, the criticism stung and hurt us. Of course, we weren't happy when the claim was originally made. And, of course, with the twenty-twenty vision that hindsight brings, it probably worked in our favour. On the one hand, we wanted to prove it was unjust. On the other, perhaps Australia began to believe there was a kernel of truth in it and we gave them a nasty jolt as a consequence.

But in truth our early form was poor and inconsistent. On any tour, there's a period of readjustment to the climate and the conditions. In Australia, where the media scrutiny is intense and the travelling can be laborious and wearing, we were out of kilter for a while. We stuttered along, unable to find our touch. Queensland skittled us for a meagre 135 before scoring 311 runs themselves. Following that, Western Australian bowled us out for 152. But I knew – as did everyone else in the touring party – that we weren't a lost cause. I only had to look around the dressing room for confirmation. We had Chris Broad, on the brink of properly establishing himself as a major batsman in the world. We had Allan Lamb and the wonderfully stylish David Gower. We had spinners of the calibre of John Embury and Phil Edmonds, who were well grooved in the business of bowling menacingly in tandem. And we had two quick bowlers capable of making Australians hop and jump: Graham Dilley and Phil DeFreitas.

And we also had a certain I T Botham, who the Australians regarded with a significant amount of respect and no little fear. They knew he could change a Test within an hour or two. We were skippered by Mike Gatting, who everyone knows liked (and still likes) a good lunch. But even more, he also relished the mental and physical demands of an Ashes series. He led us with bravado and guts. He also did one thing which in the long term counted emphatically in our favour.

On the morning of the first day of the opening Test in Brisbane, he lost the toss. After everything which had preceded it, I imagine that Gatt's mood must have been black when he came back from spinning the coin with Allan Border. I suspect he was beginning to think that Fate was going to set its face against us for the next three and a half months. If so, I remember he didn't show it. He was defiantly confident instead.

By the end of play, we'd certainly shown that we could bat. We finished on 198-2 – and I was 76 not out. I didn't add to my total – I got an inside edge to wicketkeeper Tim Zoehrer early the following morning – but 'Both' performed the only way 'Both' ever could: he attacked as if his very life depended on it. He pulled and hooked, drove and cut, hitting four sixes and 13 fours in an innings of 138 off just 174 balls. His was the major contribution to our 456 and then he chipped in with two late wickets as the Aussies were bowled out for 248. Graham Dilley finished with 5-68. We'd shown that we could bowl too.

We forced the Aussies to follow on and then bowled them out in the second innings. We knocked them over for 282 and left ourselves a modest total to chase down to win the game. I fell to Merv Hughes, who was making his Test debut. One of the things I remember most about the Test was Merv's sledging. His vocabulary – at least in my hearing – was restricted to words beginning with the letters f or c. He wasn't a happy man.

The manner of celebrations matched the style of our victory – hardly surprising, really, with Messrs Botham and Lamb taking leading roles. As we'd won, no one made a fuss about what time the party broke up.

The Brisbane Test set the positive tone for us. We drew the next two Tests and won the Fourth. The Fifth, which Australia won, proved immaterial. Gatt joined Douglas Jardine, Len Hutton, Ray Illingworth and Mike Brearley as the only England captains to have won a Test series in Australia since the Great War.

One of the reasons for our success nailed the final accusation too. We could field. In fact, we were athletic and determined. I lost count of the number of blinding catches we took. We frustrated the Aussies by diving and scrambling all over the field to stem the flow of runs. It's obvious that an Ashes series is the most important for an Englishman and an Australian. The tension, the sense of expectation and the pressure is intense. It hangs in the air. You approach it, or at least I did, with a sliver of trepidation because you don't want to let anyone down. The 86-87 tour was genuinely a great experience and the highlight of my Test career. We fully justified ourselves.

Looking back, I appreciate that I was a lucky man. I made my debut against the Aussies in the second Centenary Test at Lord's in 1980. You might not believe it, but the first Test I ever watched was the one I played in. In my teens I'd almost become a professional footballer with Jack Charlton's Middlesbrough. 'Boro is my home town and my club. My heroes in the 1970s weren't cricketers, but figures from Ayresome Park such as Graeme Souness, Bobby Murdoch, the ex-Celtic European Cup winner, and David Armstrong. I only ever saw first class cricket when Yorkshire came to Middlesbrough and I worked in the score box changing the numbers.

What struck me most about 1980 wasn't the game itself. It was the sense of occasion, which transcended the result and everything around it. Everywhere I turned, there was a face from cricket's past. It was as though someone had just opened a history book and men who'd played in Tests long ago had walked off the page. I seemed to spend most of my time signing commemorative bats, posters and photographs.

It was a privilege eight years later to get a place in the Bicentenary Test in Sydney as well. But the Test I'll always remember most of all was the one at Brisbane – the five days when we finally proved a point.

SCORECARD

Result: England won by 7 wickets

Toss: Australia, who chose to field first

Series: England led the 5-match series 1-0

Test debuts: CD Matthews (Australia);
PAJ DeFreitas and CJ Richards (England)

Player of the match: IT Botham (England)

Umpires: AR Crafter and MW Johnson

England 1st innings		RUNS
BC Broad	c Zoehrer b Reid	8
CWJ Athey	c Zoehrer b CD Matthews	76
MW Gatting	b Hughes	61
AJ Lamb	lbw b Hughes	40
DI Gower	c Ritchie b CD Matthews	51
IT Botham	c Hughes b Waugh	138
CJ Richards	b CD Matthews	0
JE Emburey	c Waugh b Hughes	8
PAJ DeFreitas	c CD Matthews b Waugh	40
PH Edmonds	not out	9
GR Dilley	c Boon b Waugh	0
Extras	(b 3, lb 19, nb 3)	25
Total	(all out; 134 overs)	456

Bowling	O	M	R	W	Econ
BA Reid	31	4	86	1	2.77
MG Hughes	36	7	134	3	3.72
CD Matthews	35	10	95	3	2.71
SR Waugh	21	3	76	3	3.61
GRJ Matthews	11	2	43	0	3.90

Fall of wickets 1-15 (Broad), 2-116 (Gatting), 3-198 (Lamb), 4-198 (Athey), 5-316 (Gower), 6-324 (Richards), 7-351 (Emburey), 8-443 (Botham), 9-451 (DeFreitas), 10-456 (Dilley)

Australia 1st innings		RUNS
GR Marsh	c Richards b Dilley	56
DC Boon	c Broad b DeFreitas	10
TJ Zoehrer	lbw b Dilley	38
DM Jones	lbw b DeFreitas	8
AR Border	c DeFreitas b Edmonds	7
GM Ritchie	c Edmonds b Dilley	41
GRJ Matthews	not out	56
SR Waugh	c Richards b Dilley	0
CD Matthews	c Gatting b Botham	11
MG Hughes	b Botham	0
BA Reid	c Richards b Dilley	3
Extras	(b 2, lb 8, w 2, nb 6)	18
Total	(all out; 104.4 overs)	248

Bowling	O	M	R	W	Econ
PAJ DeFreitas	16	5	32	2	2.00
GR Dilley	25.4	7	68	5	2.64
JE Emburey	34	11	66	0	1.94
PH Edmonds	12	6	12	1	1.00
IT Botham	16	1	58	2	3.62
MW Gatting	1	0	2	0	2.00

Fall of wickets 1-27 (Boon), 2-97 (Zoehrer), 3-114 (Jones), 4-126 (Marsh), 5-159 (Border), 6-198 (Ritchie), 7-204 (Waugh), 8-239 (CD Matthews), 9-239 (Hughes), 10-248 (Reid)

Australia 2nd innings (following on)		RUNS
GR Marsh	b DeFreitas	110
DC Boon	lbw b Botham	14
DM Jones	st Richards b Emburey	18
AR Border	c Lamb b Emburey	23
GM Ritchie	lbw b DeFreitas	45
GRJ Matthews	c & b Dilley	13
SR Waugh	b Emburey	28
TJ Zoehrer	not out	16
CD Matthews	lbw b Emburey	0
MG Hughes	b DeFreitas	0
BA Reid	c Broad b Emburey	2
Extras	(b 5, lb 6, nb 2)	13
Total	(all out; 116.5 overs)	282

Bowling	O	M	R	W	Econ
IT Botham	12	0	34	1	2.83
GR Dilley	19	6	47	1	2.47
JE Emburey	42.5	14	80	5	1.86
PAJ DeFreitas	17	2	62	3	3.64
PH Edmonds	24	8	46	1	1.91
MW Gatting	2	0	2	0	1.00

Fall of wickets 1-24 (Boon), 2-44 (Jones), 3-92 (Border), 4-205 (Ritchie), 5-224 (GRJ Matthews), 6-262 (Marsh), 7-266 (Waugh), 8-266 (CD Matthews), 9-275 (Hughes), 10-282 (Reid)

England 2nd innings (target: 75 runs)		RUNS
BC Broad	not out	35
CWJ Athey	c Waugh b Hughes	1
MW Gatting	c GRJ Matthews b Hughes	12
AJ Lamb	lbw b Reid	9
DI Gower	not out	15
Extras	(b 2, nb 3)	5
Total	(3 wickets; 22.3 overs)	77

Bowling	O	M	R	W	Econ
CD Matthews	4	0	11	0	2.75
MG Hughes	5.3	0	28	2	5.09
BA Reid	6	1	20	1	3.33
GRJ Matthews	7	1	16	0	2.28

Fall of wickets 1-6 (Athey), 2-25 (Gatting), 3-40 (Lamb)

Did not bat IT Botham, CJ Richards, JE Emburey, PAJ DeFreitas, PH Edmonds, GR Dilley

BOB APPLEYARD

Born: June 27, 1924, Wibsey, Bradford

He started as a swing and seam bowler and then developed a fast off spinner, bowling from a 16 yard run. He proved effective in any conditions. He didn't make his Yorkshire debut until 1950, but took 200 wickets the following summer (which won him *Wisden* Cricketer of the Year award). After contracting tuberculosis in 1952, an illness which threatened his life, he returned to cricket in 1954, took 154 wickets and won an England cap. He claimed 5-51 on his debut against Pakistan at Trent Bridge. In 152 first class matches, he claimed 708 wickets at 15.48. His biography, *No Coward Soul*, was named *Wisden* Book of the Year in 2004.

Test record:	
Span:	1954-1956
Matches:	9
Wickets:	31
Best bowling:	5-51
Average:	17.87
Runs:	51
Highest score:	19
	not out
Average:	17.00

Adelaide:
January 28, 29, 31, February 1, 2, 1955

Adelaide is known as The City of Churches, dominated by the spires of St Peter's Cathedral, and a place that Jack Hobbs memorably described as one of the most perfect and picturesque stages on which to bat or bowl. I remember it for an inspirational dinner with Sir Donald Bradman, who made his home there, and the compelling Test in which I came closest in my entire career to achieving total control of the ball.

For five swelteringly hot, steamy days at the beginning of 1955, I felt at my absolute peak. And we captured the Ashes for the first time since the Harlequin capped Douglas Jardine deployed the frighteningly fast Harold Larwood in the Bodyline series 22 years earlier. Adelaide was the pivotal third Test of Bodyline; Larwood struck Bert Oldfield on the head, almost caused a riot and it led to the then Australian captain Bill Woodfull uttering one of the most famous phrases in the game. 'There are two teams out there. One is playing cricket and the other is not'. For our side, captained by Len Hutton, Adelaide was the fourth Test – and we went into it, after a disastrous start to the series, leading 2-1.

Hutton's team, and the shape of the tour itself, is still talked about and discussed. It combined the flourishing bat of Denis Compton, the elegance of Peter May, the speed of Frank Tyson and the emergence of Colin Cowdrey. Australia had Neil Harvey, the always

Bob Appleyard. (YP)

flamboyant Keith Miller, Ray Lindwall, Alan Davidson and a spinner who would eventually become one of its most astute and respected captains, Richie Benaud.

It was my only tour Down Under, and the memories of it stay with me for various reasons. Firstly, because I was just relieved and glad to be alive and to be playing cricket again. In spring, 1952, I'd been diagnosed with tuberculosis. I'd walked into the hospital holding hands with my wife Connie, who was heavily pregnant. My thoracic surgeon Geoffrey Wooler gave me the grim news. 'I may have to do a little surgery'. That 'little surgery' actually lasted for six hours and meant the removal of half of my left lung. I was in bed for most of the next eleven months and I still carry a scar, which stretches from my armpit to close to my waist.

I'd taken 200 wickets in 1951, but nothing surpasses my achievement in getting fit and mentally sharp enough to return to cricket in 1954. When you've been confined to bed for what seems forever, when you've been through the dull routine of the sanatorium and when you've feared for your life and your livelihood, you can't imagine the exhilaration of the start of an English summer: the smell of the grass, the warm, fresh air and the companionship of the dressing room.

I finished my comeback season with 154 wickets and came second in the national averages (on 14.42) to Brian Statham. I bowled 1,027.3 overs, which wasn't unusual back then. My figures got me on the boat to Australia. On the way out six of the Yorkshiremen in the party – Len, Vic Wilson, Bill Bowes and Jim Kilburn (both of whom were working journalists), Abe Waddington and myself – visited Hedley Verity's grave at Caserta, which is inland from the Bay of Naples. These are the town's War Graves, and Jim called them a 'garden of smooth lawns, clean paths and simple gravestones'. Len laid a spray of white roses bound together with a Yorkshire tie. 'He said nothing,' wrote Jim 'Nothing needed to be said'. We signed the visitors' book and thought of Hedley, who, like Bill, had been part of Jardine's Bodyline tour.

We also stopped at Colombo and played a match there, which nearly ended my own tour before it began. When the game was over, the crowd spilled jubilantly on to the pitch to get close to us. One local accidentally barged into me. He ran into my left side – the area where I'd had my lung operation. I felt the sharp pain of the collision immediately. I began to fret. Frankly, I thought he'd done irreparable damage. As it turned out, I'd only cracked one of my ribs.

It meant, nonetheless, that I had to nurse myself back to fitness again and I hardly bowled early in the series as a consequence. In fact, I didn't make the First Test; partly because of my form, but mostly because Len decided he wanted a four-pronged pace attack: Messrs Tyson, Statham, Bailey and Bedser. We were mauled by an innings and 154 runs.

At first I found it hard to adapt to the Australian pitches, and the fatigue of bowling eight ball overs in crushing heat. I remember once sagging into a chair in the dressing room after a long day in the field and thinking that I wasn't fit enough to bowl in such difficult conditions. And then I looked around and saw everyone else was struggling to cope too. The sun and humidity were unrelenting. Worse, the pitches were hard and the ball didn't swing in the air. I tried to bowl too fast and my line was wrong – usually on leg stump. In the dispatches home, the reporters who accompanied us wondered whether I'd ever adjust. Eventually, I did. I slowed down and began to flight my deliveries.

I got into the second Test at Sydney, where I didn't take a wicket in seven first innings overs. In the second, I claimed Benaud (one of three occasions I'd get him out during the series) and we squeaked home by 38 runs. At Melbourne, where we won by 128 runs, my figures were two for 38 and one for 17. And so to Adelaide. . .

We lost the toss and found ourselves in the field in 90-degree heat. At the end of a painstaking first day, Australia had made 161 for four. The scoreboard – which is still in use at the Oval – recorded my name in large white letters. The figures beside it read: 11 overs, 31 runs and one wicket. That evening Colin Cowdrey and I were invited to dine with Sir Donald and Lady Bradman. He always took an interest in young cricketers or those fairly new to Test matches, and he'd asked to meet both Colin and I. To be honest, I can't remember much about the meal. I couldn't tell you what we ate or the nitty gritty of our conversation. I do remember Colin and I listened like attentive, awed apprentices as the master spoke. What I felt afterwards was that The Don had inspired me.

By lunch on the following day, my figures read: 18 overs, 42 runs and three wickets. I'd removed both the not out batsmen overnight, Benaud and Miller, and we restricted Australia to 323. It would have been far fewer if – and I still cringe when I think about it – I'd lobbed the ball cleanly back to Godfrey Evans to run out Len Maddocks with the score on 229 for eight. Instead, I threw the return so high over Godfrey's head that he'd needed to be a foot taller to take it.

We made 341 in reply, chiefly thanks to Len's 80 and Colin's 79, before I managed to find the best spell of my bowling career in Australia's second innings with three of the first four wickets, including Harvey, the dangerman. My figures then read: 12 overs, 13 runs and three wickets. Frank Tyson and Brian Statham then removed the rest. The Aussie's only made 111, which left us just 94 runs to win the match, the series and the Ashes. We nearly didn't do it.

We lurched along, like a car almost out of petrol: one for three, two for ten, three for 18 and four for 49 before Denis Compton settled us with 34 not out. The champagne flowed.

I could scarcely believe my good fortune. After the operation, and the agony and frustration of not playing at all for two seasons, I was suddenly part of an Ashes winning team – and in Australia too.

I'd visited tubercular patients in Adelaide before the Test; men who were ready to come home after their treatment. Some of them got tickets and were dotted around the ground. When I went to field near them, I'd hear the encouraging shout of 'Come on, Lofty'. I also got a letter, postmarked from England. My surgeon, Mr Wooler, had always reassured me that I'd bowl again. Now he was writing of his pride in my performances. 'I know very well,' he said 'how hard you have worked and it is a great credit to you that you have been able to stand up to so much strain'.

I couldn't have done it without him. Remarkably, we still have lunch twice a year. The latest was in early June, 2009. He is in his 98th year.

I consider myself extremely fortunate to have played in a golden era of English cricket. As my record shows, I won seven and drew two Tests – and lost none. It makes me very proud.

SCORECARD

Result: England won by 5 wickets

Toss: Australia, who chose to bat first

Series: England led the 5-match series 3-1

Umpires: MJ McInnes and RJJ Wright

Australia 1st innings		RUNS
CC McDonald	c May b Appleyard	48
AR Morris	c Evans b Tyson	25
JW Burke	c May b Tyson	18
RN Harvey	c Edrich b Bailey	25
KR Miller	c Bailey b Appleyard	44
R Benaud	c May b Appleyard	15
LV Maddocks	run out	69
RG Archer	c May b Tyson	21
AK Davidson	c Evans b Bailey	5
IWG Johnson	c Statham b Bailey	41
WA Johnston	not out	0
Extras	(b 3, lb 7, nb 2)	12
Total	(all out; 99.1 overs)	323

Bowling	O	M	R	W	Econ
FH Tyson	26.1	4	85	3	2.44
JB Statham	19	4	70	0	2.76
TE Bailey	12	3	39	3	2.43
R Appleyard	23	7	58	3	1.89
JH Wardle	19	5	59	0	2.32

Fall of wickets 1-59 (Morris), 2-86 (McDonald), 3-115 (Burke), 4-129 (Harvey), 5-175 (Benaud), 6-182 (Miller), 7-212 (Archer), 8-229 (Davidson), 9-321 (Johnson), 10-323 (Maddocks)

England 1st innings		RUNS
L Hutton	c Davidson b Johnston	80
WJ Edrich	b Johnson	21
PBH May	c Archer b Benaud	1
MC Cowdrey	c Maddocks b Davidson	79
DCS Compton	lbw b Miller	44
TE Bailey	c Davidson b Johnston	38
TG Evans	c Maddocks b Benaud	37
JH Wardle	c & b Johnson	23
FH Tyson	c Burke b Benaud	1
R Appleyard	not out	10
JB Statham	c Maddocks b Benaud	0
Extras	(b 1, lb 2, nb 4)	7
Total	(all out; 140.6 overs)	341

Bowling	O	M	R	W	Econ
KR Miller	11	4	34	1	2.31
RG Archer	3	0	12	0	3.00
IWG Johnson	36	17	46	2	0.95
AK Davidson	25	8	55	1	1.65
WA Johnston	27	11	60	2	1.66
R Benaud	36.6	6	120	4	2.44
JW Burke	2	0	7	0	2.62

Fall of wickets 1-60 (Edrich), 2-63 (May), 3-162 (Hutton), 4-232 (Compton), 5-232 (Cowdrey), 6-283 (Evans), 7-321 (Wardle), 8-323 (Tyson), 9-336 (Bailey), 10-341 (Statham)

Australia 2nd innings		RUNS
CC McDonald	b Statham	29
AR Morris	c & b Appleyard	16
JW Burke	b Appleyard	5
RN Harvey	b Appleyard	7
KR Miller	b Statham	14
LV Maddocks	lbw b Statham	2
R Benaud	lbw b Tyson	1
RG Archer	c Evans b Tyson	3
AK Davidson	lbw b Wardle	23
WA Johnston	c Appleyard b Tyson	3
IWG Johnson	not out	3
Extras	(b 4, lb 1)	5
Total	(all out; 43.2 overs)	111

Bowling	O	M	R	W	Econ
FH Tyson	15	2	47	3	2.35
JB Statham	12	1	38	3	2.37
R Appleyard	12	7	13	3	0.81
JH Wardle	4.2	1	8	1	1.41

Fall of wickets 1-24 (Morris), 2-40 (Burke), 3-54 (Harvey), 4-69 (McDonald), 5-76 (Miller), 6-77 (Benaud), 7-79 (Maddocks), 8-83 (Archer), 9-101 (Johnston), 10-111 (Davidson)

England 2nd innings (target: 94 runs)		RUNS
L Hutton	c Davidson b Miller	5
WJ Edrich	b Miller	0
PBH May	c Miller b Johnston	26
MC Cowdrey	c Archer b Miller	4
DCS Compton	not out	34
TE Bailey	lbw b Johnston	15
TG Evans	not out	6
Extras	(b 3, lb 4)	7
Total	(5 wickets; 30.4 overs)	97

Bowling	O	M	R	W	Econ
KR Miller	10.4	2	40	3	2.85
RG Archer	4	0	13	0	2.43
AK Davidson	2	0	7	0	2.62
WA Johnston	8	2	20	2	1.87
R Benaud	6	2	10	0	1.25

Fall of wickets 1-3 (Edrich), 2-10 (Hutton), 3-18 (Cowdrey), 4-49 (May), 5-90 (Bailey)

Did not bat JH Wardle, FH Tyson, R Appleyard, JB Statham

Geoffrey Boycott hits the runs for his 100th hundred. (Patrick Eagar)

GEOFFREY BOYCOTT

Born: October 21, 1940, Fitzwilliam

The most dedicated of professionals, and someone who epitomises Yorkshire grit and plain-speaking, his hunger for batting brought him 48,426 first class runs at an average of 56.83. He won every honour the game could bestow, and a following that was both loyal and devoted. His importance to England is illustrated by one statistic in particular. He played on a losing side only 20 times in 108 Tests. If he had not voluntarily made himself unavailable for Test selection during some of his peak seasons in the mid-1970s, his run scoring record would be even more impressive. He has the distinction of being the first player to receive a ball in a One Day International.

Test record:	
Span:	1964-1982
Matches:	108
Runs:	8,114
Highest score:	246
	not out
Average:	47.72
Wickets:	7
Best bowling:	3-47
Catches:	33

Headingley:
August 11, 12, 13, 15, 1977

The greatest and most memorable day of my cricketing life began bizarrely. It was 4am in a stifling hot hotel room, and I was talking to the Night Porter about the air conditioning. No matter how hard I tried, I couldn't make it work.

It was a faintly ridiculous, and certainly a surreal, situation. I knew I might be less than seven hours away from opening the batting in an Ashes Test in my own backyard. I was on 99 first class centuries. Everyone was willing me to get my hundredth hundred against Australia at Headingley, and I was uptight and tense about it. And yet, when I ought to have been fast asleep, I was embroiled in a conversation with the Night Porter about the oppressive, sticky heat.

The very idea that I could reach the landmark at Headingley seemed a fanciful notion to me. A fairytale that could never come true. Hand on heart, I didn't think I'd do it myself. One false shot, one moment of ill-luck, and the chance would be gone. As soon as I scored my 99th century at Warwickshire, just five days earlier, the hype began. Rachel, who is now my wife, told me on the 'phone:

'You've gone and done it now'.

'What do you mean?' I asked

'Everyone will expect you get your hundredth hundred at Headingley'.

I kept the Post Office busy. A stack of good luck letters, telegrams (still fashionable then) and cards began to arrive immediately. On the eve of the Test I was still trying to read, let alone reply, to all of them. During our team meeting that evening, Mike Brearley noticed I wasn't my usual self. When I asked to be excused from the general conversation, he didn't hesitate before saying yes – and he didn't need to ask why I wanted to retreat to my room.

I hoped I might effortlessly drop off to sleep after watching an hour or so of TV. Instead, I was awake and restless. I just couldn't settle. Calling the Night Porter was the last, desperate resort. I liked to have eight or eight-and-a-half hours sleep. I actually got four. I took some pills – a rare thing for me – and promptly overslept. I woke up well behind the clock, rushing rather than easing into the rhythm of my normal routine. By the time I got to Headingley, I was feeling out of sorts: weary and heavy-limbed as well as a bit flustered. The 22,000 Yorkshire crowd, however, were the polar opposite. It was a strikingly beautiful morning – warm with blue skies – and there was exuberance and a sense of anticipation hanging in the air.

I always liked to have a practice knock before an innings. This time, I barely had time to strap on my pads and get into the nets. If the truth is told, I had my fingers crossed that we'd field first. I didn't honestly feel awake enough to score runs. When Mike won the toss, and took the obvious decision to bat, I began to prepare as best I could. I knew I had to work the listlessness out of my system through force of will and concentration.

Even more responsibility rested on my shoulders when Mike was out in the opening over. But in retrospect I think his dismissal actually pushed me on. Within 20 minutes, I was a different man. I suddenly felt more relaxed and fluent. Whenever you cross the boundary rope, you're essentially on your own. In the middle no one – the press, the public or any outside influences – can reach or touch you. You're able to focus hard and purposefully on the job in the hand, which eases the tension. The first 10 to 15 runs were always the most difficult for me. Once I'd got those on the board, I thought I'd got a base on which to build. Soon I was middling the ball, and the tiredness began to drain away from me. It was replaced with a solid conviction about two things: this innings had to be treated like any other – and it had to be constructed around the basic principles I'd always employed. Play one delivery at a time; play at the tempo I felt was right for me; and play with a single-minded determination that blocked out extraneous thoughts. Whenever I played well, I took a long stride for someone who isn't terribly tall. I took a long stride that day.

Naturally the Australians tried to unnerve me. I got a jaffa from Len Pascoe, which just flicked my left wrist band and went through to Rodney Marsh. You could have heard the appeal in Sheffield. Next, I went to turn an arm ball from Ray Bright off my hip. It clipped my thigh pad and there was another shout – long and intense. Bright was positively fuming when the umpire, Bill Alley, vigorously shook his head. The captain Greg Chappell had to calm him down, and Alley moved swiftly to rebuke him too. I am sure the Aussies – and especially Bright – are still adamant that I was out on at least one of those occasions. But I know that the ball didn't get close to my bat.

In fact, I had only one moment of real trepidation. Somewhere in the 70s, I steered a short-delivery from Pascoe towards fine leg. My touch, however, was too firm. The ball went into the air and, for one awful second, I imagined Max Walker, who I knew was patrolling the area, pouching it. As I set off for the run, I waited for the crowd's reaction. If I was out, there'd be dreadful sigh followed by a funeral silence. I heard cheers instead. The ball fell short of Walker and bounced awkwardly as he went to take it. It struck his knee and flew away for four. At lunch, I'd made 35. At tea, my score had moved on to 79. With an hour left, I was on 88. On 95, the climax building, I nudged Pascoe into the covers and took a single.

What happened next – with the shadows lengthening at 5.49pm – still amazes me. I still see it in super-slow motion. And I still feel enormously grateful and privileged that Fate destined it to be so. For the record, I believe in Fate. I'm convinced some things happen for a reason.

Chappell was bowling. I kept telling myself: 'Just look for the gap around extra cover or through the on side'. In case I mistimed the ball in my enthusiasm, I was determined not to hook – even if Chappell dug one in invitingly. I'd faced 231 deliveries before Chappell came running in again. I'd struck 14 fours. The 232nd ball brought my 15th boundary - and my century.

In the millisecond it took for the ball to leave Chappell's hand, I knew the shot I'd play to it; I knew where the ball was going; I knew it would bring up my century. I saw the delivery in striking clarity, almost in High Definition. And I played it as though I was standing outside myself; actually watching myself get into position for the on-drive. I got it in the middle of the bat and I watched the ball zip past the non-striker, Graham Roope, who leapt out the way.

I remember almost instantly raising my bat and then folding my arms over my head. I remember the applause, the noise rolling down from the stands and across the pitch. And I remember realising how much it meant to me and what I'd actually achieved. I was the 18th man to score one hundred hundreds: the first to do so in a Test. The crowd came on to the pitch, wanting to pat me on the back and yell their congratulations. I can't recall what any of them said to me. I was aware, however, that I was sharing this magical hour with them – my people, my Yorkshire. There was an empathy between us. That night I rang two friends in particular: Michael Parkinson and Brian Clough. Brian's wife's Barbara said that he'd been due in a board meeting at Nottingham Forest. He phoned to tell them: 'Start without me. I'm watching my mate make history on TV'.

I might have made my 101st century in that Test too. What people tend to forget – because the hundredth hundred obscures it – is that I went on to score 191 in our total of 436 before five wickets from Ian Botham and four from Mike Hendrick bowled out the Aussies for just 103. It remains their lowest ever total in a Headingley Test. We won by an innings and 85 runs – and Derek Randall took the catch from a Rodney Marsh skier at 4.39pm on the fourth day to regain the Ashes.

We'd originally won them back on the 1970-71 tour, held on to them in 1972 and lost against the pace of Dennis Lillee and Jeff Thomson in 1975. Injury deprived me of all but two Tests in 1972, and I didn't go to Australia in '75. So the other Ashes series which sticks in my memory most strongly is 1970-71, and especially the fourth Test at Sydney. I batted as well there as I've ever done in my life.

The series was a meandering, inconclusive affair until Sydney. The first two Tests at Brisbane and Perth were drawn. The third, at Melbourne, was abandoned on the third day without a ball bowled. But sparks from the Sydney Test set things ablaze, and enabled us to make history. In those days, I regarded the pitch at the SCG as one of the finest in the world. It was shorn of grass and consequently had plenty of pace and bounce for the quick bowlers. As matches wore on, it also had enough in it for the spinners, who got good turn.

The game was pure theatre – captivating, absorbing cricket from first to last ball. As well as my own innings, it stands out because I'd never seen John Snow bowl better or more fiercely. He made a good length ball ride up uncomfortably into the ribs. Snow was nasty and dangerous, and the Aussies couldn't handle him. Basil D'Oliveira also made a critical half century in our second innings, which merely emphasised his unflappability under pressure. He demonstrated a cool head – a calm, easy temperament, which he exuded whenever he came down the steps and through the pavilion gate.

After winning the toss, we made 332. Johnny Gleeson and Ashley Mallett claimed eight of our wickets – a sure sign of the quality of the pitch. The Aussies replied with 236 and it was my job to build on the lead. The surface was wearing, the spinners were wily and crafty and I had to watch each ball with a hawk-like eye. I made 142 not out in our total of 319 for five declared. I felt then, as I do now, that it was technically one of my most accomplished innings. With D'Oliveira, who hit 56, we put ourselves into the box seat.

The Aussies crumbled to Snow, who claimed seven for 40 and cut the ball brilliantly off the seam. He almost single-handedly dismissed them for a paltry 116, which gave us a huge winning margin: 299 runs – the largest England victory against Australia since Freddie Brown's tourists beat Donald Bradman and company by more than 300 at Brisbane in late 1937.

Before we left England, no one gave us much of a chance of beating Australia. Only Douglas Jardine (with Bodyline) in 1932-33 and Len Hutton in 1954-55 had returned as Ashes winning captains. Ray Illingworth joined the pantheon. To win the Ashes is one thing. To win them in Australia was truly an incredible, exhilarating feeling. We didn't, however, come home to ticker-a-tape parades and gongs at Buckingham Palace. While the country was ecstatic, and we were lauded as heroes, I recall that our perk was being invited down to Taylor's of London, where each of us received a bottle of vintage port with our names on the bottle.

Geoff Boycott is congratulated immediately after scoring his 100th hundred. (YP)

Celebrations, as Boycott is mobbed by supporters. (YP)

SCORECARD

Result: England won by an innings and 85 runs

Toss: England, who chose to bat first

Series: England led the 5-match series 3-0

Umpires: WE Alley and WL Budd

England 1st innings		*RUNS*
JM Brearley	c Marsh b Thomson	0
G Boycott	c Chappell b Pascoe	191
RA Woolmer	c Chappell b Thomson	37
DW Randall	lbw b Pascoe	20
AW Greig	b Thomson	43
GRJ Roope	c Walters b Thomson	34
APE Knott	lbw b Bright	57
IT Botham	b Bright	0
DL Underwood	c Bright b Pascoe	6
M Hendrick	c Robinson b Pascoe	4
RGD Willis	not out	5
Extras	(b 5, lb 9, w 3, nb 22)	39
Total	(all out; 155.4 overs)	436

Bowling	O	M	R	W	Econ
JR Thomson	34	7	113	4	3.32
MHN Walker	48	21	97	0	2.02
LS Pascoe	34.4	10	91	4	2.62
KD Walters	3	1	5	0	1.66
RJ Bright	26	9	66	2	2.53
GS Chappell	10	2	25	0	2.50

Fall of wickets 1-0 (Brearley), 2-82 (Woolmer), 3-105 (Randall), 4-201 (Greig), 5-275 (Roope), 6-398 (Knott), 7-398 (Botham), 8-412 (Underwood), 9-422 (Hendrick), 10-436 (Boycott)

Australia 1st innings		*RUNS*
RB McCosker	run out	27
IC Davis	lbw b Hendrick	0
GS Chappell	c Brearley b Hendrick	4
DW Hookes	lbw b Botham	24
KD Walters	c Hendrick b Botham	4
RD Robinson	c Greig b Hendrick	20
RW Marsh	c Knott b Botham	2
RJ Bright	not out	9
MHN Walker	c Knott b Botham	7
JR Thomson	b Botham	0
LS Pascoe	b Hendrick	0
Extras	(lb 3, w 1, nb 2)	6
Total	(all out; 31.3 overs)	103

Bowling	O	M	R	W	Econ
RGD Willis	5	0	35	0	7.00
M Hendrick	15.3	2	41	4	2.64
IT Botham	11	3	21	5	1.90

Fall of wickets 1-8 (Davis), 2-26 (Chappell), 3-52 (McCosker), 4-57 (Hookes), 5-66 (Walters), 6-77 (Marsh), 7-87 (Robinson), 8-100 (Walker), 9-100 (Thomson), 10-103 (Pascoe)

Australia 2nd innings (following on)		*RUNS*
RB McCosker	c Knott b Greig	12
IC Davis	c Knott b Greig	19
GS Chappell	c Greig b Willis	36
DW Hookes	lbw b Hendrick	21
KD Walters	lbw b Woolmer	15
RD Robinson	b Hendrick	20
RW Marsh	c Randall b Hendrick	63
RJ Bright	c Greig b Hendrick	5
MHN Walker	b Willis	30
JR Thomson	b Willis	0
LS Pascoe	not out	0
Extras	(b 1, lb 4, w 4, nb 18)	27
Total	(all out; 89.5 overs)	248

Bowling	O	M	R	W	Econ
RGD Willis	14	7	32	3	2.28
M Hendrick	22.5	6	54	4	2.36
AW Greig	20	7	64	2	3.20
IT Botham	17	3	47	0	2.76
RA Woolmer	8	4	8	1	1.00
DL Underwood	8	3	16	0	2.00

Fall of wickets 1-31 (Davis), 2-35 (McCosker), 3-63 (Hookes), 4-97 (Walters), 5-130 (Chappell), 6-167 (Robinson), 7-179 (Bright), 8-244 (Walker), 9-245 (Thomson), 10-248 (Marsh)

Ray Illingworth at the end of the 1968 Headingley test match with Australia. In the background is Tom Graveney, England's acting captain. (YP)

RAY ILLINGWORTH

Born: June 8, 1932, Pudsey

One of the most tactically astute men ever to captain England, he led them on 21 occasions. He won 12 Tests, drew 14 and lost only five. He also captained England during their series against the Rest of the World. With Yorkshire, he won every honour imaginable, including the County Championship seven times. He won it again with unfashionable and unfancied Leicestershire, and also steered them to two John Player Sunday League titles and two Benson and Hedges Cups. In his first class career, he scored almost 25,000 runs and took more than 2,000 wickets. Later he became England's Chairman of Selectors and manager for three years.

Test record:	
Span:	1958-1973:
Matches:	61
Runs:	1,836
Highest score:	113
Average:	23.24
Wickets:	122
Best bowling:	6-29
Average:	31.20
Catches:	45

Sydney:
February, 12, 13, 14, 16, 17, 1971

I was fortunate. I came from an era in which cricketing knowledge was passed down from one Yorkshire generation to the next – from Wilfred Rhodes and George Hirst to Johnny Wardle and Brian Close. When I first came into the dressing room, I had to 'sit and say nowt'. But if you wanted to learn – and provided you were prepared to keep your eyes and ears wide open – you could always pick up something new about the game almost every day merely by listening and watching.

It was the start of a long process, which eventually turned me into an England captain. It also carried me to the pinnacle of my career – the 1970-71 Ashes series in Australia. As a skipper, I prided myself on two things. The first was honesty. I never knowingly lied to a player. Barry Dudleston, who I played alongside at Leicestershire, once said: 'If Illy stabbed you, he always stabbed you in the chest'. It's true, and I took his observation about me as a compliment. If I ever had anything to say to a player, I said it to his face and not behind his back. The second attribute was tactical awareness. It stemmed directly from my early days at Yorkshire, where I picked up so much from the experienced pros, and then throughout the late 1950s and 1960s when I became established in the team and made Test appearances.

Put it this way. When a batsman came down the steps, my field would already be set specifically for him. I'd know his strengths, his foibles and his weaknesses. If he was new to the game, I'd know them within five overs. I like to think my knowledge and preparation was part of the reason why we beat Australia.

There were some formidably high hurdles to clear along the way. Believe it or not, my hardest job before setting off was to convince the selectors that Basil D'Oliveira should go on the tour. When we came to pick the side, there must have been a dozen of us sitting around the table, including the vice-captain Colin Cowdrey. To be frank, I didn't think Cowdrey should have been there. He'd skippered the team in the West Indies, and had found it hard to manage Basil, who I think 'enjoyed' himself a little too much for Cowdrey's liking. Cowdrey argued that we shouldn't take Basil. Eventually, I ended the discussion with a simple but firm declaration: 'If Basil doesn't go, I don't go'. I'd promised Basil he would tour because I thought we needed him. If I'd backed down, I wouldn't have been able to look him in the eyes again. Suffice to say in the Tests, Basil scored nearly 400 runs, took six wickets and caused me no trouble whatsoever. He would have done anything for me.

I gave the Australian newspapers a headline on our arrival – and I meant it too. I said we'd got two of the best fast bowlers in the world in John Snow and Alan Ward (who was actually faster than Snow). I added that: 'If the wickets are right, we'll bowl you out'. The predictable headlines followed. My strategy had to change very early on because Ward, who was always fragile, got injured. We had to fly in a replacement for him, and so we called up 19-year-old Bob Willis. I hadn't seen Willis, who was then at Surrey. But John Edrich, who had played alongside him, reassured me. 'He won't let you down. He'll make it bounce'. He was absolutely right. Willis made his debut in the fourth Test and bowled with some real fire for us.

I like to think that I knew how to handle fast bowlers. Remember, in 1970-71 we bowled eight ball overs in Tests in Australia. In the intense heat, it was necessary to look after and nurture the bowlers such as Snow, Willis, Peter Lever and Ken Shuttleworth. At the end of the series, Willis' father came up to me and said that his son had learnt more in the past few months than at any other stage of his career. And when the dust of the series had settled, Frank Tyson wrote a perceptive piece in which he said I'd used my fast bowlers sympathetically. He said that they'd thank me for my field placings too. I knew what he meant. The Aussies were a tough team with seasoned and talented players, among them Keith Stackpole, the captain, Bill Lawry and, of course, the emerging Chappell brothers, Ian and Greg. I also paid special attention to someone who never did particularly well in England, but was a fluent, dangerous batsman in his home conditions: Doug Walters. He scored quickly too, and could soon turn a match in their favour. We worked on Walters and gave him short balls, which he cut or steered to backward of point or towards third man – and got out. In fact, third man became a wicket-taking position for us for several batsmen. It merely emphasises the importance of knowing how your opponent plays.

We weren't really fancied to win; probably because we hadn't beaten Australia out there since Len Hutton's tour in 1954-55. In fact, the first question I got in Australia came from E W Swanton, who was the doyen of the correspondents and a firm 'establishment' figure. He asked: 'Would you be prepared to leave yourself out of the side if you weren't doing well?' He was so blunt because he wanted Cowdrey – not me – as captain. I said I thought it was an unfair question, but I gave him the answer he wanted nonetheless. 'Yes,' I told him.

We started slowly. Our warm-up games were affected by the weather and the fact we lost the toss, consequently spending a lot of time in the field. In fact, at one stage Geoff Boycott retired hurt so someone else could get into the middle. Going in to the first Test at Brisbane, I thought we needed one more match to get ourselves properly sharp. We still nearly won it – despite the fact the Aussies were 372 for two at one stage in their first innings. I went into the match with four main bowlers – myself and Derek Underwood as spinners, Shuttleworth and Snow as the quicks. I also had D'Oliveira for a bit of medium pace. Snow took six for 114 as we eventually bowled them out for 433. The last eight wickets fell for 61. We made 464 and then hit them again. This time Shuttleworth took five for 47 and the Aussies made only 214. We lost precious time through heavy rain. When the covers were taken off, the excess water fell on the bowlers' run ups – and we lost more time. Otherwise, we'd have led the series from the off. We moved to Perth for the first Test ever played there. It was another high-scoring affair. The Aussies replied to our 397 with 440, including 171 from Ian Redpath. The match, however, was nearly always destined for the draw it became.

The third Test at Melbourne was totally washed out. It did contain one highlight. The ex-Australian skipper Ian Johnson, who was secretary of Melbourne Cricket Club, said the pitch was fit to play – despite the fact it had been pouring like Noah's flood. He decided to walk out to the wicket in his best suit. He slipped and fell on his backside. He came into the Pavilion covered in black soil. 'Is it still alright out there, Ian?' we asked him innocently.

Finally we took the lead at Sydney, where Snow was at his irresistible best. There was always something in the pitch there. I liked the SCG because it was a true contest between bat and ball, which is the way I like cricket to be played. If you scored over 300, you'd done well. Snow didn't merely get the ball to rear up chest high. He also got it to move appreciably off the seam as it arrowed towards the batsmen's breast bone. I was fortunate to play with some great fast bowlers, including Fred Trueman. But I'm sure no one could have bowled better than Snow that day. He was unplayable, and took seven for 40 in the second innings. We crushed the Aussies by 299 runs. I always remember one thing about the match. During the tea break, I called the team together in the dressing room and told them to imagine we were in the Gillette Cup Final at Lord's and that the opposition needed eight runs to win off the last over. I asked them to think about how they'd be feeling, and how they'd approach the challenge. My trick worked. We played with so much intensity that we rolled the Aussies over in half an hour.

Next, at Melbourne again, we got the greenest track we'd seen in Australia. It was so emerald that Lever came on off his shorter, 'Sunday League' run up because he thought he'd get more seam. Australia, who scored 493 in the first innings, batted on too long in the second, finally declaring at 169 for four. We were in trouble because we were two batsmen down: D'Oliveira was limping and Brian Luckhurst had broken his thumb. We clung on thanks to two unbeaten 70s from Boycott and Edrich.

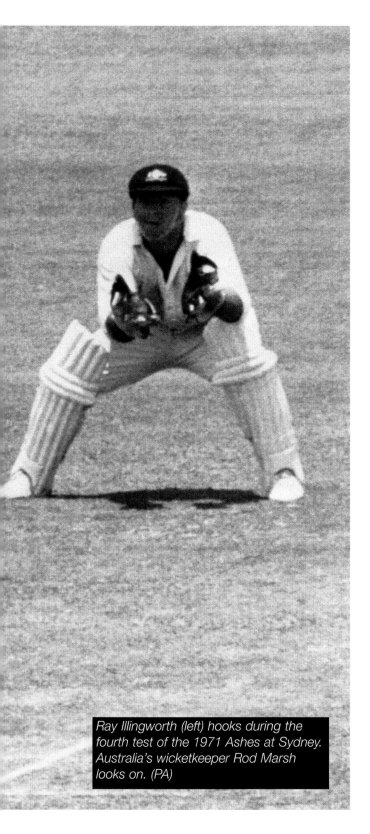

Ray Illingworth (left) hooks during the fourth test of the 1971 Ashes at Sydney. Australia's wicketkeeper Rod Marsh looks on. (PA)

At Adelaide, we had the Aussies on the run, and I could have forced the follow on. I didn't because Snow was weary. The Melbourne Test had finished just three days earlier and he'd already lost about half a stone in weight in the extreme heat. What is more, Lever had a sore shoulder and I was carrying a slight hamstring. If we bowled again, I thought we'd genuinely struggle.

Back in Sydney, Australia panicked in an effort to level things up and retain the Ashes. They changed their captain, sacking Lawry and appointing Ian Chappell. I've always thought they made a mistake in not retaining Lawry as a batsman. He was a difficult man to get out at the best of times. Once, his off stump was flattened and he simply stood on the spot, as though reluctant to walk off. 'Come on Bill,' I said 'The pole's on the ground . . . you've got to go!'

It had been raining for two days before the start, and Ian won the toss and put us in. With our bowling attack, I'm not exaggerating when I say that we'd have skittled them out for less than 80 if we'd been fielding first. We did really well to get 184. The rest is Ashes history. With eight wickets down, I was seriously thinking of declaring. There was only half an hour's play left, and I wanted to get at Australia because I knew the pitch would play far differently the following morning. We were polished off before I had to make that choice – and then we knocked over their two openers before stumps. On the first day, the outfield was long and lush. You couldn't really hit a four. On the second, with the Aussies batting, there were three mowers cutting it as smooth as a bowling green.

Sydney became notorious because of

my decision to lead the team off the field after Snow was pelted with missiles and beer cans on the boundary. One drunken fan yanked him by the shirt. Snow had hit Terry Jenner on the head with a bouncer, and the crowd didn't like it. I had no option but to head for the dressing room. I was genuinely worried about what might happen to him – and to the rest of us – if things got really ugly. We'd already gone into the match without Boycott, who had his arm in a sling. When Snow fractured and dislocated his right little finger, after colliding with the fence, we'd lost two of our most effective players. I have to say that I don't think I've seen Geoff in better form. He finished the series with 657 runs and an average of 93.85. Snow was slowing down because he'd worked so hard, but his psychological effect on the Aussies was immense. Thankfully, we won by 62 runs after bowling them out for only 160. I felt relief as much as elation.

People tend to forget some important factors about the series. Foremost among them was the change in the lbw laws in 1970. For the first time, a batsman couldn't be out if the ball pitched outside off-stump and he was playing a shot. It sounds implausible, but we went through six Tests without getting a single lbw decision. Can you imagine any team today beating Australia in a long, hard series without being awarded a solitary leg before? No, neither can I. It had never happened before – and it hasn't happened since. I'm not saying that we didn't have legitimate shouts. But we certainly didn't get any to go our way.

During the fourth Test – the first ever played at Perth – I also told our team not to walk unless the umpire gave them out. Keith Stackpole clearly gloved a catch and acted as though nothing had happened. In fact, there were about half a dozen decisions – nicks and fine edges – which went for him. In the first Test, he somehow managed to avoid being run out too. Boycott threw down the stumps and a photograph in the newspapers revealed the truth. The bails were a foot in the air . . . and Stackpole's bat was a yard out of his ground. I ought to add that he was, and remains, a good friend of mine.

The atmosphere was always good between the teams. At the end of every day's play, we had a beer together. At one stage, the man who looked after the Sydney dressing room came in late at night to find a group of us there, including myself, Edrich, Stackpole and Dennis Lillee. 'Aren't you lot going to bugger off home,' he said. We were enjoying ourselves so much that we didn't want to go anywhere.

Despite our win, we were hardly given much of a fanfare on arriving home. I remember the celebratory dinner at Lord's. I sat next to Micky Stewart. It was such a flat, muted occasion that Micky turned to me at one point and said jokingly: 'You did win the Ashes, didn't you?'

We did – and we deserved them too.

SCORECARD

Result: England won by 62 runs

Toss: Australia, who chose to field first

Series: England won the 7-match series 2-0 (1 abandoned)

Test debuts: AR Dell and KH Eastwood (Australia)

Umpires: TF Brooks and LP Rowan

England 1st innings		RUNS
JH Edrich	c GS Chappell b Dell	30
BW Luckhurst	c Redpath b Walters	0
KWR Fletcher	c Stackpole b O'Keeffe	33
JH Hampshire	c Marsh b Lillee	10
BL D'Oliveira	b Dell	1
R Illingworth	b Jenner	42
APE Knott	c Stackpole b O'Keeffe	27
JA Snow	b Jenner	7
P Lever	c Jenner b O'Keeffe	4
DL Underwood	not out	8
RGD Willis	b Jenner	11
Extras	(b 4, lb 4, w 1, nb 2)	11
Total	(all out; 76 overs)	184

Bowling	O	M	R	W	Econ
DK Lillee	13	5	32	1	1.84
AR Dell	16	8	32	2	1.50
KD Walters	4	0	10	1	1.87
GS Chappell	3	0	9	0	2.25
TJ Jenner	16	3	42	3	1.96
KJ O'Keeffe	24	8	48	3	1.50

Fall of wickets 1-5 (Luckhurst), 2-60 (Edrich), 3-68 (Fletcher), 4-69 (D'Oliveira), 5-98 (Hampshire), 6-145 (Knott), 7-156 (Snow), 8-165 (Illingworth), 9-165 (Lever), 10-184 (Willis)

Australia 1st innings		RUNS
KH Eastwood	c Knott b Lever	5
KR Stackpole	b Snow	6
RW Marsh	c Willis b Lever	4
IM Chappell	b Willis	25
IR Redpath	c & b Underwood	59
KD Walters	st Knott b Underwood	42
GS Chappell	b Willis	65
KJ O'Keeffe	c Knott b Illingworth	3
TJ Jenner	b Lever	30
DK Lillee	c Knott b Willis	6
AR Dell	not out	3
Extras	(lb 5, w 1, nb 10)	16
Total	(all out; 83.6 overs)	264

Bowling	O	M	R	W	Econ
JA Snow	18	2	68	1	2.83
P Lever	14.6	3	43	3	2.18
BL D'Oliveira	12	2	24	0	1.50
RGD Willis	12	1	58	3	3.62
DL Underwood	16	3	39	2	1.82
R Illingworth	11	3	16	1	1.09

Fall of wickets 1-11 (Eastwood), 2-13 (Stackpole), 3-32 (Marsh), 4-66 (IM Chappell), 5-147 (Walters), 6-162 (Redpath), 7-178 (O'Keeffe), 7-195* (Jenner, retired not out), 8-235 (Lillee), 9-239 (GS Chappell), 10-264 (Jenner)

England 2nd innings		RUNS
JH Edrich	c IM Chappell b O'Keeffe	57
BW Luckhurst	c Lillee b O'Keeffe	59
KWR Fletcher	c Stackpole b Eastwood	20
JH Hampshire	c IM Chappell b O'Keeffe	24
BL D'Oliveira	c IM Chappell b Lillee	47
R Illingworth	lbw b Lillee	29
APE Knott	b Dell	15
JA Snow	c Stackpole b Dell	20
P Lever	c Redpath b Jenner	17
DL Underwood	c Marsh b Dell	0
RGD Willis	not out	2
Extras	(b 3, lb 3, nb 6)	12
Total	(all out; 100.7 overs)	302

Bowling	O	M	R	W	Econ
DK Lillee	14	0	43	2	2.30
AR Dell	26.7	3	65	3	1.81
KD Walters	5	0	18	0	2.70
TJ Jenner	21	5	39	1	1.39
KJ O'Keeffe	26	8	96	3	2.76
KH Eastwood	5	0	21	1	3.15
KR Stackpole	3	1	8	0	2.00

Fall of wickets 1-94 (Luckhurst), 2-130 (Fletcher), 3-158 (Edrich), 4-165 (Hampshire), 5-234 (Illingworth), 6-251 (D'Oliveira), 7-276 (Knott), 8-298 (Lever), 9-299 (Underwood), 10-302 (Snow)

Australia 2nd innings (target: 223 runs)		RUNS
KH Eastwood	b Snow	0
KR Stackpole	b Illingworth	67
IM Chappell	c Knott b Lever	6
IR Redpath	c Hampshire b Illingworth	14
KD Walters	c D'Oliveira b Willis	1
GS Chappell	st Knott b Illingworth	30
RW Marsh	b Underwood	16
KJ O'Keeffe	c sub (K Shuttleworth) b D'Oliveira	12
TJ Jenner	c Fletcher b Underwood	4
DK Lillee	c Hampshire b D'Oliveira	0
AR Dell	not out	3
Extras	(b 2, nb 5)	7
Total	(all out; 62.6 overs)	160

Bowling	O	M	R	W	Econ
JA Snow	2	1	7	1	2.62
P Lever	12	2	23	1	1.43
BL D'Oliveira	5	1	15	2	2.25
RGD Willis	9	1	32	1	2.66
DL Underwood	13.6	5	28	2	1.52
R Illingworth	20	7	39	3	1.46
KWR Fletcher	1	0	9	0	6.75

Fall of wickets 1-0 (Eastwood), 2-22 (IM Chappell), 3-71 (Redpath), 4-82 (Walters), 5-96 (Stackpole), 6-131 (Marsh), 7-142 (GS Chappell), 8-154 (O'Keeffe), 9-154 (Lillee), 10-160 (Jenner)

Arnie Sidebottom – June 1985. (YP)

ARNIE SIDEBOTTOM

Born: April 1, Shawlands, Barnsley, 1954

He took 596 first class wickets in a career spanning from 1973 to 1991 and finished with an average of 24.42. He also played for Manchester United, Huddersfield and Halifax. Although a lower order batsmen, his career includes a first class century – 124 against Glamorgan in 1977.

Test record:	
Span:	1985
Matches	1
Runs	2
Wickets	1 (65)
Highest Score	2

Trent Bridge:
July 11, 12, 13, 15, 16, 1985

I have to be perfectly honest. I shouldn't have been picked for what turned out to be my one and only Test. From the early 1970s to 1980, I'd played professional sport solidly for 12 months each and every year: football for Manchester United, Huddersfield or Halifax during the winter and cricket for Yorkshire during the summer.

By now I was 31 and well past my sell by date as a front line seamer. My body – especially my toes, the soles of my feet and my knees – had taken too much punishment, and the accumulated physical wear and tear of being both a footballer and a cricketer was beginning to take its toll. I was nursing various, niggling injuries and trying to pretend that nothing hurt when, in actual fact, everything did: joints and muscles, bones and nerve ends. Some of the tackles I'd made (and received) as a defender – during a period in which referees were more forgiving of the rough stuff – and the daily pounding of running in and bowling had made me a bit brittle by the time I unexpectedly got the call to go to Trent Bridge.

We didn't have a sophisticated system, either at Test or County level, for treating injuries. There were no team doctors or personal trainers to wrap you in cotton wool or to advise you on how to treat strains or slight pulls, which might get worse if you ignored the warning signs. You were your own physician and you had to heal yourself as best you could. You strapped up your own ankles. You arranged your ice bath after the game – if you could find enough ice and enough gallons of cold water. You didn't get a rub down after a long day in the field. A sportsman nonetheless knows his own body and general condition. When England wanted me, I knew I wasn't tip-tip; not remotely so, in fact.

Although I'd given up football in 1980 because Yorkshire made it clear that I couldn't carry on combining the two sports, I was still pushing myself to the maximum. Of course, Yorkshire were right. The two seasons were beginning to seriously overlap on one another. Now football is virtually played during all but one month of the year and Test and One Day Internationals fill the calendar. No one could do what I and others like me – Phil Neale, Jim Cumbs, Chris Balderstone, for example – used to take for granted.

I'd reached the stage at which I could just about cope with County Cricket. A Test, however, was something different. Given my circumstances, I was staggered that England wanted me at all. I'd recently taken four for 70 against Worcestershire at Harrogate (as it turned out, these were my best figures for the summer), but I can't say my form was gold standard.

As for the Test itself, I can only describe it quite genuinely as 'naff'. Our team contained some of the finest players of the age: Gooch, Gower and Botham in particular, with whom it was a privilege to share a dressing room. But the five days produced a tame, listless draw on a tame, listless pitch. Trent Bridge was a lively place in the County Championship during this period – and that is putting it very mildly. Usually, the only way you could distinguish the track from the outfield was by watching where the umpires stuck in the stumps. Notts were a hard, exceptionally competitive team led by Clive Rice and supported by Richard Hadlee. That new ball combination was deadly, and the pitches were specifically prepared to suit them – grassy and emerald green so deliveries jagged about and batsmen frequently found it difficult to get into double figures, let alone go on to build big scores.

It was far different for the Test. The pitch was benign, bleached almost white and shorn as close as a man with a bald pate. We won the toss and made 456. Australia chalked up more than 500. For me, it was a total let down.

I bowled just 18.4 overs – taking my one and only Test wicket when I trapped Bob Holland lbw – before I stumbled in one of the footholds at the pavilion end and broke my big toe. I was soon hobbling around like an invalid. A bowler who can't bowl is like a pub with no beer. There isn't much point to him. And I felt a bit like a spare part. I left Nottingham knowing in my own mind that my Test 'career' had come and gone in an eye blink.

I've still never minded the tag of 'One cap wonder'. There are lots of players who might have played for England, but who for one reason or another didn't get the chance. I can always say I was an England player, however briefly, and I was given a sweater, a cap and a number to prove it.

We all think about the 'what ifs' in our lives and the paths we could have taken; the might have beens and maybes. If I hadn't gone on the 1982 'rebel' tour to South Africa, I could well have played far more Tests for England. I'd taken 62 wickets in the summer before heading off for South Africa without crossing the radar of England's selectors. I felt I had an obligation to my family – Ryan was only two years old then – to earn more money for a handful of games than I could make in an entire football and cricket season combined. It was the right decision. I thought so then – and I think so now.

I had a glorious sporting life. Aged 17, I made my debut for Manchester United at Old Trafford in front of 66,000. I'd never be afraid of the size of any crowd again. We played Sheffield United with a forward line so good that you catch your breath as you recite it: Willie Morgan, George Best, Bobby Charlton, Denis Law, Brian Kidd.

Best was unquestionably the best player I ever saw or played alongside. He was a genius, a word I don't use blithely or loosely. You'd have to sell the entire, present-day Leeds team to afford his wages. He was that good.

And now I take immense pride in watching Ryan. Not, I hasten to add, that I've watched him very much because I get too nervous. To tell the truth, I'm far more nervous for him than I ever was for myself. When he bowls, I bowl every ball with him.

Last winter he paid for my wife Gillian and I to go to New Zealand. I was able to watch him in a Test for the first time. I sat in absolute rapture as he removed first Stephen Fleming, then Matthew Sinclair and finally Jacob Oram – and became only the 11th England bowler to take a hat-trick. It doesn't get any better than that . . .

SCORECARD

Result: Match drawn

Toss: England, who chose to bat first

Series: 6-match series level 1-1

Test debut: A Sidebottom (England)

Player of the match: DI Gower (England)

Umpires: DJ Constant and AGT Whitehead

England 1st innings		RUNS
GA Gooch	c Wessels b Lawson	70
RT Robinson	c Border b Lawson	38
DI Gower	c Phillips b O'Donnell	166
MW Gatting	run out	74
AJ Lamb	lbw b Lawson	17
IT Botham	c O'Donnell b McDermott	38
PR Downton	c Ritchie b McDermott	0
A Sidebottom	c O'Donnell b Lawson	2
JE Emburey	not out	16
PH Edmonds	b Holland	12
PJW Allott	c Border b Lawson	7
Extras	(lb 12, w 1, nb 3)	16
Total	(all out; 129.4 overs)	456

Bowling	O	M	R	W	Econ
GF Lawson	39.4	10	103	5	2.59
CJ McDermott	35	3	147	2	4.20
SP O'Donnell	29	4	104	1	3.58
RG Holland	26	3	90	1	3.46

Fall of wickets 1-55 (Robinson), 2-171 (Gooch), 3-358 (Gatting), 4-365 (Gower), 5-416 (Lamb), 6-416 (Botham), 7-419 (Downton), 8-419 (Sidebottom), 9-443 (Edmonds), 10-456 (Allott)

Australia 1st innings		RUNS
GM Wood	c Robinson b Botham	172
AMJ Hilditch	lbw b Allott	47
RG Holland	lbw b Sidebottom	10
KC Wessels	c Downton b Emburey	33
AR Border	c Botham b Edmonds	23
DC Boon	c & b Emburey	15
GM Ritchie	b Edmonds	146
WB Phillips	b Emburey	2
SP O'Donnell	c Downton b Botham	46
GF Lawson	c Gooch b Botham	18
CJ McDermott	not out	0
Extras	(b 6, lb 7, w 2, nb 12)	27
Total	(all out; 201.2 overs)	539

Bowling	O	M	R	W	Econ
IT Botham	34.2	3	107	3	3.11
A Sidebottom	18.4	3	65	1	3.48
PJW Allott	18	4	55	1	3.05
PH Edmonds	66	18	155	2	2.34
JE Emburey	55	15	129	3	2.34
GA Gooch	8.2	2	13	0	1.56
MW Gatting	1	0	2	0	2.00

Fall of wickets 1-87 (Hilditch), 2-128 (Holland), 3-205 (Wessels), 4-234 (Border), 5-263 (Boon), 6-424 (Wood), 7-437 (Phillips), 8-491 (Ritchie), 9-539 (O'Donnell), 10-539 (Lawson)

England 2nd innings		RUNS
GA Gooch	c Ritchie b McDermott	48
RT Robinson	not out	77
DI Gower	c Phillips b McDermott	17
MW Gatting	not out	35
Extras	(b 1, lb 16, nb 2)	19
Total	(2 wickets; 68 overs)	196

Bowling	O	M	R	W	Econ
GF Lawson	13	4	32	0	2.46
CJ McDermott	16	2	42	2	2.62
RG Holland	28	9	69	0	2.46
SP O'Donnell	10	2	26	0	2.60
GM Ritchie	1	0	10	0	10.00

Fall of wickets 1-79 (Gooch), 2-107 (Gower)

Did not bat AJ Lamb, IT Botham, PR Downton, A Sidebottom, JE Emburey, PH Edmonds, PJW Allott

CHRIS SILVERWOOD

Born: March 5, 1975, Pontefract

A winner of the Denis Compton award in 1996, he is approaching 600 first class wickets. He helped Yorkshire win the County Championship in 2001, and moved from Headingley to Middlesex at the end of the 2005 summer.

Test record:	
Span:	1996-2002
Matches:	6
Wickets:	11 (best 5/91)
Average:	40.36
Runs:	29
Highest score:	10
Average:	7.25
Catches:	2

Perth:
November 29, 30, December 1, 2002

My insight into the real nature of Ashes battles curiously came with the bat rather than the ball. I actually spent more time at the crease in my one and only Test against Australia – at Perth in 2002 – than I did trying to use my speed against Langer, Hayden, Ponting, Waugh and company.

I remember batting in the first innings against Brett Lee. The WACA was a belting pitch. It was pale and shorn of grass, which created genuine pace for the quicks. But it also meant the ball came on for the batsmen too. Shots could be made with real conviction and purpose. There was no nervousness about the odd delivery keeping low or embarrassing you with irregular bounce.

Fast bowlers have always relished Perth: Lillee and Thomson, Holding and Marshall and, further back, Trueman and Snow. Lee's tail was certainly up on this track. He was lethal, and I'm an archetypal tail-ender in Test terms. I was number ten, just ahead of Steve Harmison, who would never call himself a run-maker.

I'm not exaggerating when I say I could barely see most of the balls Lee bowled at me. Less than half a second after release, it seemed to land in Adam Gilchrist's hands with a loud thud. Above all, I remember one particular ball. He bowled me an especially nasty

Australia's Jason Gillespie (right) celebrates the wicket of England's Chris Silverwood, during the first day of the third 'Ashes' Test at the WACA cricket ground. England were all out for 185, Australia finished the day on 126-2. (PA)

bouncer, and I somehow weaved and ducked out of the way of it. When I glanced across at the electronic gauge, which was measuring his speed, I could hardly believe the illuminated figure: 96.5mph

I know this will sound a rather strange reaction, but I actually started to laugh. It seemed ridiculous that I was in the middle of a Test match, bat in hand, trying to protect my wicket against someone who was firing the ball at me almost as though it was a military shell.

My early Ashes memories were all about Ian Botham – one of my heroes – and the '81 Headingley Test. I was too young to take much notice, or absorb the significance of his performance when he pulled off his extraordinary feat of single-handedly saving England and then, against all the odds, actually winning it for them. But I caught up with it on video and I've watched it time and again ever since. It still makes compelling viewing.

After Lee bowled that ball, I thought to myself: 'Well, welcome to Ashes cricket at last'. It put 'Both's' feat into even clearer perspective – and his greatness too. Darren Lehmann was fielding close beside me. When he saw I was laughing, he began to laugh too. We both saw the surreal side of things.

Lee fininished with figures of three for 78. For the record, I wasn't one of his victims. I eventually got out to Jason Gillespie for 10, including a solitary four. But that single moment against Lee summed up the fierce intensity of the Ashes for me. It personified the needle and niggle, the nerves, the high quality of the Tests and the pure theatre which is England v Australia (or vice versa). As for Lee . . . well, I think Michael Vaughan believes that he'd never seen him bowl as fast as he did that day.

We lost the Test by an innings and 48 runs to an Australian side that was ruthless and remarkable. The experience is so vivid, I can still see Lee tearing in towards me. I can still picture the crowd as I walked out to bowl myself, and feel the atmosphere of the occasion too. And I can still hear the sledging in both ears from the Aussies. To paraphrase Dickens: It was the best of times, and it was the worst of times for me.

It was the best because I shouldn't have been playing at all. I wasn't picked for the tour. I was actually playing in the Hong Kong Sixes tournament – and doing well – when I got a call from David Graveney. 'Don't get too comfortable out there,' he said. 'You're coming to Australia'. Simon Jones had been injured in Brisbane, and I was drafted in as his replacement.

I arrived shortly before a match in Hobart and ended up as 12th man. I found myself in the Test team two weeks later. I barely had time to unpack my case, though. The Aussie strategy was always to target one bowler. As I was essentially the 'new boy' – though I'd played five Tests previously, four of them against South Africa – I knew I'd be the guy in the firing line. As it turned out, the Aussies didn't get the chance to challenge me.

That's why the Test was also the worst of times. When I came on to bowl, I damaged my foot after only seven deliveries. As I came up to bowl the first ball of my second over, my left boot collapsed inwards at the very point of impact. I fell to the ground. Within a few minutes, my ankle was the size of a football. 'Are you OK?' Alec Stewart asked, already knowing the answer. Afterwards, I watched a replay of what happened to me. It was a real horror show. I winced when I saw the acute and awkward angle that my foot eventually ended up in.

I managed to get through four overs for 29 runs. My pace, which began around 90mph, fell to 80mph or slightly lower. There was nothing I could do. I couldn't run hard at all. The Aussies made 456 and then completed a fairly straightforward win by dismissing us for 223.

I was back in England for Christmas – after less than four weeks with the party. I knew I'd have to fly home because the ankle could only heal through prolonged rest. The scan I was given shortly afterwards confirmed it. At the time, though, I felt dreadful. I'd come so far, broken into the side through someone else's misfortune and then lost it through a slice of my own. In retrospect, I can't really complain. At least I played in an Ashes Test.

At 17, I'd gone to South Africa with Yorkshire to learn the game. I watched Craig McDermott bowl against them. He was actually due to come to Headingley as our overseas player, but the deal fell through. I studied him, and greatly admired the way he bowled. I said two things to myself – and to a friend. 'I want to play in an Ashes Test . . . and I want to play at Newlands in a Test too'. My friend thought I was slightly mad. In 2000, I took five for 91 at Newlands against South Africa in the Fourth Test.

So I'm grateful to have been able to fulfil my other goal at Perth. However brief, it was still an Ashes appearance.

SCORECARD

Result: Australia won by an innings and 48 runs

Toss: England, who chose to bat first

Series: Australia led the 5-match series 3-0

Player of the match: DR Martyn (Australia)

Umpires: SA Bucknor (West Indies) and RE Koertzen (South Africa)

TV umpire: DJ Harper

Match referee: Wasim Raja (Pakistan)

England 1st innings		RUNS
ME Trescothick	c Gilchrist b Lee	34
MP Vaughan	c Gilchrist b McGrath	34
MA Butcher	run out (Waugh)	9
N Hussain	c Gilchrist b Lee	8
RWT Key	b Martyn	47
AJ Stewart	c Gilchrist b McGrath	7
C White	c Martyn b Lee	2
AJ Tudor	c Martyn b Warne	0
RKJ Dawson	not out	19
CEW Silverwood	c Hayden b Gillespie	10
SJ Harmison	b Gillespie	6
Extras	(lb 2, nb 7)	9
Total	(all out; 64.2 overs; 295 mins)	185

Bowling	O	M	R	W	Econ
GD McGrath	17	5	30	2	1.76
JN Gillespie	17.2	8	43	2	2.48
B Lee	20	1	78	3	3.90
SK Warne	9	0	32	1	3.55
DR Martyn	1	1	0	1	0.00

Fall of wickets 1-47 (Trescothick, 12.4 ov), 2-69 (Butcher, 18.5 ov), 3-83 (Hussain, 20.6 ov), 4-101 (Vaughan, 29.3 ov), 5-111 (Stewart, 37.6 ov), 6-121 (White, 43.3 ov), 7-135 (Tudor, 46.6 ov), 8-156 (Key, 52.5 ov), 9-173 (Silverwood, 60.1 ov), 10-185 (Harmison, 64.2 ov)

Australia 1st innings		RUNS
JL Langer	run out (Silverwood/ Stewart)	19
ML Hayden	c Tudor b Harmison	30
RT Ponting	b White	68
DR Martyn	c Stewart b Tudor	71
DS Lehmann	c Harmison b White	42
SR Waugh	b Tudor	53
AC Gilchrist	c Tudor b White	38
SK Warne	run out (Harmison/Tudor)	35
B Lee	c Key b White	41
JN Gillespie	b White	27
GD McGrath	not out	8
Extras	(b 4, lb 5, nb 15)	24
Total	(all out; 99.1 overs; 436 mins)	456

Bowling	O	M	R	W	Econ
CEW Silverwood	4	0	29	0	7.25
AJ Tudor	29	2	144	2	4.96
SJ Harmison	28	7	86	1	3.07
C White	23.1	3	127	5	5.48
MA Butcher	10	1	40	0	4.00
RKJ Dawson	5	0	21	0	4.20

Fall of wickets 1-31 (Langer, 5.3 ov), 2-85 (Hayden, 12.6 ov), 3-159 (Ponting, 34.2 ov), 4-226 (Lehmann, 51.2 ov), 5-264 (Martyn, 62.6 ov), 6-316 (Gilchrist, 72.1 ov), 7-348 (Waugh, 81.2 ov), 8-416 (Warne, 92.4 ov), 9-423 (Lee, 95.2 ov), 10-456 (Gillespie, 99.1 ov)

England 2nd innings		RUNS
ME Trescothick	c Gilchrist b Lee	4
MP Vaughan	run out (Lee/ Gilchrist/McGrath)	9
RKJ Dawson	c Waugh b Gillespie	8
MA Butcher	lbw b McGrath	0
N Hussain	c Gilchrist b Warne	61
RWT Key	lbw b McGrath	23
AJ Stewart	not out	66
C White	st Gilchrist b Warne	15
AJ Tudor	retired hurt	3
SJ Harmison	b Lee	5
CEW Silverwood	absent hurt	-
Extras	(b 8, lb 5, w 1, nb 15)	29
Total	(all out; 82.1 overs; 377 mins)	223

Bowling	O	M	R	W	Econ
B Lee	18.1	3	72	2	3.96
GD McGrath	21	9	24	2	1.14
JN Gillespie	15	4	35	1	2.33
SK Warne	26	5	70	2	2.69
DR Martyn	2	0	9	0	4.50

Fall of wickets 1-13 (Trescothick, 6.4 ov), 2-33 (Dawson, 12.6 ov), 3-34 (Vaughan, 15.5 ov), 4-34 (Butcher, 15.6 ov), 5-102 (Key, 50.6 ov), 6-169 (Hussain, 69.4 ov), 7-208 (White, 77.5 ov), 7-214* (Tudor, retired not out), 8-223 (Harmison, 82.1 ov)

Richard Dawson bowling on day 2 in Adelaide. (Patrick Eagar).

RICHARD DAWSON

Born: August 4, 1980, Doncaster

He was an integral part of Yorkshire's Championship winning team in 2001 and won himself a reputation as a rising star, which led to an early England call-up. At the end of 2007, he moved to Northamptonshire and then on to Gloucestershire. He has taken almost 200 first class wickets.

Test record:	
Span:	2001-2003
Matches:	7
Wickets:	11
Best bowling:	4-134
Average:	61.54
Runs:	114
Highest score:	19
	not out
Average:	11.40
Catches:	3

Adelaide:
November 21, 22, 23, 24, 2002

I owe one of my five Ashes wickets to Shane Warne, who virtually talked me through how to take it.

I'd already played in three Tests in India during the previous winter. When I was chosen for the 2002-03 tour to Australia, however, I didn't expect to figure in the team. Ashley Giles was the first choice spinner, and would certainly have remained so – if Steve Harmison's pace hadn't broken his wrist during practice just two days before Adelaide. It was the second Test, and we'd been crushed in the opening one by 384 runs at Brisbane. With Giles out, I was suddenly and unexpectedly in.

At least we won the toss and Michael Vaughan batted gloriously to make 177 in our total of 342. He'd go on to score 633 runs at 63.30 and win England's Player of the Series award. I was out for six, trapped lbw to Warne. I'll always remember waiting to go into bat. At Adelaide, the crowd are on top of the play because the boundaries either side of the wickets – especially near the Pavilion – are fairly tight. The grassy bank, as well as the perimeters, were choked with people and the atmosphere was unbelievably tense. I don't like hanging around. I prefer to be straight on the field rather than watching. But I was in good company. As well as Michael Vaughan and I, Craig White and Matthew Hoggard were both in the team.

Of course, Australia were a quite brilliant, dazzling side; strong throughout with Justin Langer and Matthew Hayden as openers, Ricky Ponting at three, Steve Waugh at five, Yorkshire's then overseas player, Darren Lehmann, at six and Adam Gilchrist to follow. They were so fluent and formidable that at times you couldn't bowl to them. You had to wait until they made a mistake, which often took a long time coming. The bowling – especially with Warne and Glen McGrath and a fit-again Brett Lee later on – was positively awesome. The most daunting thing was that if one of them fell out of form (a rare occurrence) or dropped out through injury, there were always two – and sometimes three – players waiting to slide seamlessly into the order. It proves one thing: it is easier to fit into a winning side.

Australia replied in style at Adelaide, putting 552 on the ancient but impressive scoreboard on the ground. I'd already got Langer, who was caught behind by Alec Stewart. Later in the innings, I was wheeling away as usual, trying to work out through intuition how to remove the likes of Ponting (154) and Damien Martyn (95) when I started to get a lot of useful advice in my ear.

Warne was the non-striker and he started to give me some tips about tactics and pace and variation in my bowling. It must have worked because the next wicket I claimed was Warne's own. I caught and bowled him for 25. He drove the ball straight back at me.

At the end of the Test, which we lost by an innings and 51 runs, Lehmann asked Warne to have another word with me. He spent a lot of time talking about good spin bowling – the preparation for it, the shrewdness of it, and ways in which I might improve. I could hardly believe his generosity. When Warne made his impossible-to-forget impact on the Ashes – bowling Mike Gatting with that ball at Old Trafford – I was only 13 years old and studying for my GCSE exams. To be honest, I remember him more in the next home series four years later, even though I watched Tim May, an off-spinner like me, with far closer attention. I'd started my career in England juniors as a batsman who also bowled medium pace. But I always knew I wasn't a seamer. Eventually I turned to spin instead and really only watched matches when a spinner came on. Now, here I was – in the thick of an Ashes series – getting my own personal tutorial from the most talked about spinner in the modern game. It summed up Warne as a very decent bloke. In the intense heat of competition, he could easily have said nothing to me.

Of course, I was still learning my trade. In 2001, I'd taken 30 wickets in Yorkshire's Championship winning summer. I'd only recently left University and I thought the year was almost ruined when I broke my hand. When July came, and I got my chance at last, everything clicked. I took 30 wickets in nine matches – and finished as our third most successful wicket-taker behind Steve Kirby on 47 and Chris Silverwood, who took 33. My performance got me on the Indian and New Zealand tour at only 22 years old.

I relished India. There was no real pressure and I was bowling well and freely. In Australia, it was much different and far more competitive. The pressure never eased. No matter where you went, the talk was all about the Ashes. There was no escape and never any peace. Even in the nets at Adelaide, the crowd was constantly on your back.

We lost heavily at Perth in the next Test. Chris Silverwood and I share the same memory of Brett Lee – albeit I had the rather more painful experience. I was padded up as nightwatchman at the end of the second day. I kept glancing at the TV screen checking Lee's pace. As he limbered up, it went from fast to very fast to almost super-sonic. When Marcus Trescothick was out, I went down the Pavilion steps feeling what I can only describe as an amalgam of eager anticipation and utter, absolute terror. The light was fading. I had to protect Michael Vaughan. And Lee was sensing blood – mine! With his first ball, he bowled me a bouncer, which clipped my shoulder. About three days later, my shoulder had virtually seized up. I couldn't lift my arm to bowl and my bruise was a sight to behold. I spent the next two weeks receiving treatment on it. There were about seven overs left, and I managed to survive at least three of them against Lee. When I came off beside Michael, the Barmy Army were chanting and I had the widest smile you can ever imagine on my face. Somehow, I'd come through it.

To play at Melbourne on Boxing Day was another remarkable experience. Nearly 200,000 people in total saw the five days as Australia won – yet again – by five wickets. In my seven Tests for England, we won only once. It came in the final Test at Sydney, and I'll never forget the exhilaration of it. I also got Damien Martyn, caught behind by Alec Stewart.

I still came home from Australia without much confidence. As a result, the 2003 summer came and went miserably for me. A lot of people during the tour had begun pointing out things that were either wrong with my bowling or needed improvement. Nothing had been said when I'd been doing well. I suppose I listened to too many voices at once and didn't follow my gut instincts. Really, I should have just stuck at my own game and ignored most of what was being said to me. But that is something you only learn as you get older . . .

Having said all that, I wouldn't have missed Australia for anything. However mentally and physically tiring the tour became, it was one of those experiences to cherish. I'm so grateful to have been a part of it.

SCORECARD

Result: Australia won by an innings and 51 runs

Toss: England, who chose to bat first

Series: Australia led the 5-match series 2-0

Player of the matchL: RT Ponting (Australia)

Umpires: SA Bucknor (West Indies) and RE Koertzen (South Africa)

TV umpire: SJ Davis

Match referee: Wasim Raja (Pakistan)

England 1st innings

England 1st innings		RUNS
ME Trescothick	b McGrath	35
MP Vaughan	c Warne b Bichel	177
RWT Key	c Ponting b Warne	1
N Hussain	c Gilchrist b Warne	47
MA Butcher	c Gilchrist b Gillespie	22
AJ Stewart	lbw b Gillespie	29
C White	c Bichel b Gillespie	1
RKJ Dawson	lbw b Warne	6
AR Caddick	b Warne	0
MJ Hoggard	c Gilchrist b Gillespie	6
SJ Harmison	not out	3
Extras	(lb 7, nb 8)	15
Total	(all out; 115.5 ov; 484 mins)	342

Bowling	O	M	R	W	Econ
GD McGrath	30	11	77	1	2.56
JN Gillespie	26.5	8	78	4	2.90
AJ Bichel	20	2	78	1	3.90
SK Warne	34	10	93	4	2.73
SR Waugh	5	1	9	0	1.80

Fall of wickets 1-88 (Trescothick, 21.2 ov), 2-106 (Key, 30.6 ov), 3-246 (Hussain, 72.4 ov), 4-295 (Vaughan, 89.3 ov), 5-295 (Butcher, 92.4 ov), 6-308 (White, 96.6 ov), 7-325 (Dawson, 108.6 ov), 8-325 (Caddick, 110.4 ov), 9-337 (Stewart, 115.1 ov), 10-342 (Hoggard, 115.5 ov)

Australia 1st innings

Australia 1st innings		RUNS
JL Langer	c Stewart b Dawson	48
ML Hayden	c Caddick b White	46
RT Ponting	c Dawson b White	154
DR Martyn	c Hussain b Harmison	95
SR Waugh	c Butcher b White	34
DS Lehmann	c sub (A Flintoff) b White	5
AC Gilchrist	c Stewart b Harmison	54
SK Warne	c & b Dawson	25
AJ Bichel	b White	48
JN Gillespie	not out	0
Extras	(b 1, lb 17, w 7, nb 18)	43
Total	(9 wickets dec; 139.2 overs; 594 mins)	552

Did not bat GD McGrath

Bowling	O	M	R	W	Econ
AR Caddick	20	2	95	0	4.75
MJ Hoggard	26	4	84	1	3.23
SJ Harmison	28.2	8	106	2	3.74
C White	28	2	106	4	3.78
RKJ Dawson	37	2	143	2	3.86

Fall of wickets 1-101 (Hayden, 18.3 ov), 2-114 (Langer, 21.4 ov), 3-356 (Martyn, 99.5 ov), 4-397 (Ponting, 105.1 ov), 5-414 (Lehmann, 111.4 ov), 6-423 (Waugh, 113.4 ov), 7-471 (Warne, 124.5 ov), 8-548 (Bichel, 138.5 ov), 9-552 (Gilchrist, 139.2 ov)

England 2nd innings

England 2nd innings		RUNS
ME Trescothick	lbw b Gillespie	0
MP Vaughan	c McGrath b Warne	41
MA Butcher	lbw b McGrath	4
N Hussain	b Bichel	10
RWT Key	c Lehmann b Bichel	1
AJ Stewart	lbw b Warne	57
C White	c sub (B Lee) b McGrath	5
RKJ Dawson	c Gilchrist b McGrath	19
MJ Hoggard	b McGrath	1
SJ Harmison	lbw b Warne	0
AR Caddick	not out	6
Extras	(b 3, lb 4, nb 8)	15
Total	(all out; 59.2 overs; 257 mins)	159

Bowling	O	M	R	W	Econ
GD McGrath	17.2	6	41	4	2.36
JN Gillespie	12	1	44	1	3.66
SK Warne	25	7	36	3	1.44
AJ Bichel	5	0	31	2	6.20

Fall of wickets 1-5 (Trescothick, 1.4 ov), 2-17 (Butcher, 2.3 ov), 3-36 (Hussain, 11.2 ov), 4-40 (Key, 13.3 ov), 5-114 (Vaughan, 36.2 ov), 6-130 (White, 47.6 ov), 7-130 (Stewart, 48.1 ov), 8-132 (Hoggard, 51.1 ov), 9-134 (Harmison, 52.6 ov), 10-159 (Dawson, 59.2 ov)

MARTYN MOXON

Born: May 4, 1960, Stairfoot, Barnsley

He made his Yorkshire debut in 1981 and collected two centuries in his opening two home matches. He went on to score more than 21,000 first class runs, including 45 hundreds and 116 half centuries. Named Wisden Cricketer of the Year in 1993, he has coached both Durham and Yorkshire.

Test record:	
Span:	1986-1989
Matches:	10
Runs:	455
Highest score:	99
Average:	28.43
Catches:	10

Sydney:
January 29, 30, 31; February 1, 2, 1988

Nothing prepared me for the build up to the Bicentenary Test. As well as the pageant surrounding the occasion – the legends invited to watch it and the significance of the contest itself – I found myself, on the opening morning, standing on the outfield listening to the National Anthems. It completely threw me out of my normal stride.

Like a lot of cricketers, I relied heavily on routine and superstition throughout my playing days. I had a set way of getting ready to bat. Left pad on first. Check and re-check everything. Get my mind focussed. I didn't like to be interrupted or disrupted. The need to line up and listen, as God Save the Queen was tannoyed across the Sydney Cricket Ground, scrambled my thoughts. I stood there very proud but also quite emotional. I was already padded up too. But Chris Broad and I still had to go out for the ceremony, and then return to the dressing room after it was over. We only had ten minutes or so to settle ourselves again before walking out for the serious business of trying to score some runs.

It was my first Test against Australia, but I'd slept well the night before. Apart from the butterflies which accompanied me before any innings, I didn't feel much apprehension — either on the way to the SCG or when we reached it. The preamble changed everything. By the time I'd heard the anthems, my nerves were on edge. My head was full of it, rather

Moxon v New Zealand 88
(Patrick Eagar)

than the bowling I was about to face. In fact, I'd never been so nervous before (and I'd never be as nervous again on the field). As I felt rushed, I honestly didn't feel ready to bat.

It meant that the first hour was frankly an act of pure survival on my part. I scratched around, straining to get some fluency and to feel at home. I managed it through a sheer act of will and a bit of luck too; Allan Border dropped me in the slips off Steve Waugh. Slowly, I started to middle the ball. Our opening partnership began to slip into gear. We passed 50 and were beginning to approach our century stand. I struck Peter Sleep for an impressive four and thought I'd got through a difficult spell. I'd reached 40, and now there was something for me to build on. And then, believe it or not, Sleep bowled me a full toss. The ball came to me at a lower trajectory than I imagined it would. I tried to whip it through midwicket, but ended up playing both over and across it. I heard the terrible click and clatter of my stumps. I was so annoyed with myself. Having done the hard, grinding work, I'd let myself down with a piece of awful misjudgement.

At least we made 425 in our first innings and then bowled out the Aussies for 214, forcing them to follow on. We just couldn't press home the massive advantage we'd given ourselves. David Boon was at his pugnacious best. I don't think he offered a chance, or played a false shot, in his 184. The match ended tamely in a draw.

I had to wait more than 18 months for my next chance against Australia – my one and only Test in an Ashes series. It was a peculiar and desperate summer for England. I'd seen nothing but the highlights and quick snatches of the action on TV. We'd lost the first Test by 210 runs, the next by six wickets and the fourth by nine wickets. The third had been drawn.

The selectors' indecision was fatal. I can put it into perspective with two statistics. I was the 22nd player called up to the face Australia – and England used 29 in total in six Tests. No sooner did someone get in than the axe fell and another batsman (or bowler) was thrown in. As the series neared its end, I was selected for the first time since the West Indies demolished us the previous season. I don't know why the call up came, except that it must have been my turn. Although I passed 1,000 runs, I hadn't been in prime form: 21 and 25 against Middlesex at Headingley; 18 and 53 in the match against Northamptonshire at Abbeydale Park; 10 and 34 against Warwickshire at Edgbaston.

What came next rates as one of my worst experiences. Australia made 602 and bowled us out for 255. I faced three balls before I played forward to Terry Alderman and nicked it to Steve Waugh at third slip. The follow on was grimmer; much grimmer, actually. Even to this day – because I've never asked him – I don't know why David Gower decided to promote himself to open the second innings and drop me to number five. But it shattered my confidence and left my preparation in disarray. I felt as though he didn't have any faith in me, so I didn't have any faith in myself as a consequence. I wasn't the only batsmen to have failed in the first innings: Mike Atherton survived only two balls; Gower himself made just 11; Tim Curtis was out for 2.

It felt as if I was being singled out, and I didn't know how to cope with it emotionally or practically. Like any opener, I wasn't used to filling in time before batting. I didn't know whether to watch the match unfold or to find a quiet corner and sit by myself. By the time I got in we were already 67-3. Gower's experiment didn't work either. He survived six balls for five runs. Alderman got me again. The delivery kept a little low and bowled me for 18. We were crushed by an innings, and I never played in a Test match again.

It's terribly ironic, really. I was at my peak in the years that followed – specifically between 1990 and 1995 – and yet I didn't get another chance to prove it. I was certainly more accomplished technically – especially off the back foot, where previously I'd tended to try to hit the ball too hard and often got myself out as a result. (Steve Oldham was particularly helpful in improving that aspect of my game). More importantly, I became stronger mentally too. In that period, a player generally had to sort out his own problems. Today players have access to a sports psychologist if necessary.

At Trent Bridge, I felt isolated and alone. I should have been thinking how I could bat, but a sense of inferiority had taken over. Things could have turned out differently for me. I could have got two back-to-back Test centuries.   In Auckland, a month after the Bicentenary Test, I was out on 99 against New Zealand – the day after I'd struck a delivery in the middle of the bat and the umpire called my 'runs' as 'leg byes'. More disappointingly, I was unbeaten on 81 in the next Test against New Zealand at Wellington when rain came in and washed the match away. I needed someone – anyone – to remind me of those Tests at Trent Bridge when I was feeling so low and disorientated. A year or two later, I'd have coped much better with Gower's decision.

I might still not have understood it, though.

SCORECARD

Result: Match drawn

Toss: England, who chose to bat first

Series: 1987/88 Bicentenary Test drawn

Player of the match: DC Boon (Australia)

Umpires: AR Crafter and PJ McConnell

England 1st innings

		RUNS
BC Broad	b Waugh	139
MD Moxon	b Sleep	40
RT Robinson	c Veletta b Dodemaide	43
MW Gatting	c Dyer b Waugh	13
CWJ Athey	c & b Taylor	37
DJ Capel	c Sleep b Taylor	21
JE Emburey	st Dyer b Sleep	23
BN French	st Dyer b Taylor	47
NA Foster	c Border b Taylor	19
EE Hemmings	not out	8
GR Dilley	b Waugh	13
Extras	(b 4, lb 9, w 1, nb 8)	22
Total	(all out; 172.5 overs)	425

Bowling	O	M	R	W	Econ
CJ McDermott	35	8	65	0	1.8
AIC Dodemaide	36	10	98	1	2.72
PL Taylor	34	10	84	4	2.47
SR Waugh	22.5	5	51	3	2.23
PR Sleep	45	8	114	2	2.53

Fall of wickets 1-93 (Moxon), 2-192 (Robinson), 3-245 (Gatting), 4-262 (Broad), 5-313 (Athey), 6-314 (Capel), 7-346 (Emburey), 8-387 (Foster), 9-410 (French), 10-425 (Dilley)

Australia 1st innings

		RUNS
DC Boon	c French b Foster	12
GR Marsh	c French b Capel	5
DM Jones	c Emburey b Hemmings	56
AR Border	c Broad b Capel	2
MRJ Veletta	c Emburey b Hemmings	22
SR Waugh	c French b Dilley	27
PR Sleep	c Athey b Foster	41
GC Dyer	lbw b Dilley	0
PL Taylor	c French b Hemmings	20
AIC Dodemaide	not out	12
CJ McDermott	c Foster b Dilley	1
Extras	(lb 10, w 1, nb 5)	16
Total	(all out; 96.1 overs)	214

Bowling	O	M	R	W	Econ
GR Dilley	19.1	4	54	3	2.81
NA Foster	19	6	27	2	1.42
JE Emburey	30	10	57	0	1.90
DJ Capel	6	3	13	2	2.16
EE Hemmings	22	3	53	3	2.40

Fall of wickets 1-18 (Boon), 2-25 (Marsh), 3-34 (Border), 4-82 (Veletta), 5-116 (Jones), 6-147 (Waugh), 7-153 (Dyer), 8-183 (Taylor), 9-209 (Sleep), 10-214 (McDermott)

Australia 2nd innings (following on)

		RUNS
DC Boon	not out	184
GR Marsh	c Athey b Emburey	56
DM Jones	c Moxon b Capel	24
AR Border	not out	48
Extras	(b 3, lb 7, nb 6)	16
Total	(2 wickets; 135 overs)	328

Bowling	O	M	R	W	Econ
GR Dilley	13	1	48	0	3.69
NA Foster	15	6	27	0	1.80
JE Emburey	38	5	98	1	2.57
DJ Capel	17	4	38	1	2.23
EE Hemmings	52	15	107	0	2.05

Fall of wickets 1-162 (Marsh), 2-218 (Jones)

Did not bat MRJ Veletta, SR Waugh, PR Sleep, GC Dyer, PL Taylor, AIC Dodemaide, CJ McDermott

John Hampshire (PA)

JOHN HAMPSHIRE

Born: February 10, 1941, Thurnscoe

He captained Yorkshire during a period of upheaval between 1979-80 and finally moved to Derbyshire, where he played for three seasons. His batting career brought 28,059 runs in first class matches and 446 catches. He became an umpire in 1985 and was appointed to the Test list four years later. In 1999, he joined the ICC panel of umpires and retired from the County circuit in 2005.

Test record:	
Span:	1969-75
Matches:	8
Runs:	403
Highest score:	107
Average:	26.86
Catches:	9

Headingley:
August, 14, 15, 16, 18, 19, 1975

What I'm about to say isn't false modesty, but plain fact. The truth is that I never thought I was good enough to be a Test cricketer. I was a good, solid player. But you need something more – a special ingredient – to prosper at Test level, and I always felt that I didn't have it. Of course, I always wanted to be a Test player – but I didn't want to fail in the challenge either.

I got my first chance against the West Indies in 1969. I was 12th man in the first Test at Old Trafford and my most significant job was to run from dressing room to pitch and discreetly pass Tom Graveney an important piece of kit that he'd forgotten in the rush to get ready to face Garry Sobers and Vanburn Holder, who was making his debut. Tom wasn't wearing his box. I arrived with it tucked in my trouser pocket.

The next Test was at Lord's and I expected to do 12th man tasks again. But as I walked into the ground, past the well-wishers at the Grace Gates, I came across Geoff Boycott, who merely said: 'Congratulations. You're in'.

On the first morning, after we'd lost the toss and been put into the field, I couldn't bring myself to put on my new England sweater. The crown and three lions just didn't seem right on my chest. I didn't think I was worthy enough to wear them. I'd grown up in the

1975 Headingley Test "George Davis is innocent protest" (YP)

era of Len Hutton, and afterwards there were batsmen of the pedigree of Peter May, Ted Dexter and Ken Barrington. These names were icons to me. But who was I? Just a lad from Thurnscoe. I could never shake off the thought that I was lucky to be in the England side – and that I didn't necessarily deserve the honour.

When we batted, I became the first England batsman to score a century on his debut at Lord's – 107 – and I had the added, glorious bonus of reaching it on the Saturday in front of a full house. I also achieved it with a hairline fracture of my forearm, which I suffered during the Test, and another hairline fracture of the little finger of my left hand, which had been caused by a ball from Mike Procter six days earlier on a difficult wicket at Middlesbrough.

I played the next Test against the West Indies at Headingley before being dropped for the series against New Zealand, which immediately followed it. I don't think I would have gone on the 1970-71 Ashes tour without the influence of Ray Illingworth, who captained the side. I'm sure Ray's support was responsible for getting me into the party.

I already knew Australia and the Australians, and that fact was probably uppermost in Ray's mind too. I wouldn't need much time to acclimatise. For three years, starting in 1967, I coached in Tasmania. I was the State's first coach since the 1920s when, ironically, another Yorkshireman called Hughie Myers was given the post. I had to build up the structure from scratch – though I'm not sure at first whether some of the Tasmanians were grateful to be told what to do by a 'whinging Pom'. By the second year, I was regularly working 12 hour days and I also managed to hit good scores, including 80 and one hundred against the touring Indians. By the third, I was captain of the State side and I struck 120 against the West Indies, including a six against Charlie Griffith that went clean out of the ground. Griffith had struck me on the temple in a match at Middlesbrough in 1963 and I was taken off on a stretcher. For years, I never had a full night's sleep as a consequence. That moment marked a turning point in my career. On many occasions at the wicket, I couldn't maintain my concentration. I am convinced that ball from Griffith was responsible for it.

To win the Ashes in Australia is every Englishman's ambition, and I'm proud to say I played a part in it, albeit a small one. As 12th man at Perth, I'd come on and taken two close catches to remove first Keith Stackpole and then Ian Chappell in the Australian second innings. The Aussie captain Bill Lawry was furious because he thought I was a specialist catcher, and that we'd broken an 'unwritten rule' that said 12th men should be placed in the outfield, not close to the bat.

I played in the last two Tests in Adelaide and Sydney, where we clinched the series. At Adelaide, there was a young, quick bowler making his debut. His name was Dennis Lillee. Even then, it was obvious that Lillee would become one of the great quicks. He had skill as well as raw pace and energy. Within two years, no one was faster than him. I made 55 before flicking at a leg-side ball from Greg Chappell and holing out to Lillee at long leg. I was angry with myself because I'd got through what I believed was the hard part of my innings. I'd been able to temporarily tame the spinner Johnny Gleeson, who I had never previously picked.

When we won in Sydney – quite easily as it turned out – we went to an impromptu party on the coast. It lasted well into the early hours. We were still bleary eyed and clutching our sore heads as we climbed on the plane for the next stage of the tour in New Zealand. In those days, we spent around six and a half months away from home and you had to be tough and strong willed to survive it.

Although I played against Australia at the Oval in 1972, making 42 in the first innings and 20 in the second, I didn't get the chance to face them again until one of the most infamous Tests in English cricket history in 1975.

It was played at Headingley and heading towards a good finish on the last day. I made just 14 in our total of 288 and was caught for nought off Jeff Thomson in the second. The Aussies found themselves needing 200 or so to win with seven wickets left. And then the most incredible thing happened.

I'd been to hospital for an X-ray on a finger, which I'd damaged in the field. When I arrived at Headingley, and walked into the dressing room, I was amazed to find that no one else was changed – or was even making an attempt to get changed. I sat down next to my kit and started to put on my whites. 'What are you doing?' I was asked. 'I'm going for a net,' I replied.

Only at that point did I find out the truth. The match had been abandoned. Four vandals had broken into the ground the previous night, moved the covers and dug up part of the pitch on a length at the rugby end. They also poured oil on it. It was a protest against the conviction of a man called George Davis, a minicab driver who had been jailed for his part in an armed robbery.

When I heard about the abandonment, I didn't honestly know what to do. It left a terrible, hollow feeling in my stomach.

I never played for England again. Although I had no personal problems with the skipper Tony Greig, I made it clear that I didn't think it was a good idea to give the captaincy to someone born in another country. Greig was civil, polite and helpful to me. But I think, perhaps rightly, he felt that he couldn't have someone in his team who held such views.

It was a strange, slightly sad way to say goodbye to Test cricket.

SCORECARD

Result: Match drawn

Toss: England, who chose to bat first

Series: Australia led the 4-match series 1-0

Test debut: PH Edmonds (England)

Umpires: DJ Constant and AE Fagg

England 1st innings		RUNS
B Wood	lbw b Gilmour	9
JH Edrich	c Mallett b Thomson	62
DS Steele	c Walters b Thomson	73
JH Hampshire	lbw b Gilmour	14
KWR Fletcher	c Mallett b Lillee	8
AW Greig	run out	51
APE Knott	lbw b Gilmour	14
PH Edmonds	not out	13
CM Old	b Gilmour	5
JA Snow	c Walters b Gilmour	0
DL Underwood	c GS Chappell b Gilmour	0
Extras	(b 4, lb 15, w 11, nb 9)	39
Total	(all out; 101.2 overs)	288

Bowling	O	M	R	W	Econ
DK Lillee	28	12	53	1	1.89
JR Thomson	22	8	53	2	2.40
GJ Gilmour	31.2	10	85	6	2.71
MHN Walker	18	4	54	0	3.00
IM Chappell	2	0	4	0	2.00

Fall of wickets 1-25 (Wood), 2-137 (Edrich), 3-159 (Hampshire), 4-189 (Fletcher), 5-213 (Steele), 6-268 (Greig), 7-269 (Knott), 8-284 (Old), 9-284 (Snow), 10-288 (Underwood)

Australia 1st innings		RUNS
RB McCosker	c Hampshire b Old	0
RW Marsh	b Snow	25
IM Chappell	b Edmonds	35
GS Chappell	c Underwood b Edmonds	13
R Edwards	lbw b Edmonds	0
KD Walters	lbw b Edmonds	19
GJ Gilmour	c Greig b Underwood	6
MHN Walker	c Old b Edmonds	0
JR Thomson	c Steele b Snow	16
DK Lillee	b Snow	11
AA Mallett	not out	1
Extras	(lb 5, w 1, nb 3)	9
Total	(all out; 76.5 overs)	135

Bowling	O	M	R	W	Econ
JA Snow	18.5	7	22	3	1.16
CM Old	11	3	30	1	2.72
AW Greig	3	0	14	0	4.66
B Wood	5	2	10	0	2.00
DL Underwood	19	12	22	1	1.15
PH Edmonds	20	7	28	5	1.40

Fall of wickets 1-8 (McCosker), 2-53 (Marsh), 3-78 (GS Chappell), 4-78 (Edwards), 5-81 (IM Chappell), 6-96 (Gilmour), 7-104 (Walker), 8-107 (Walters), 9-128 (Lillee), 10-135 (Thomson)

England 2nd innings		RUNS
B Wood	lbw b Walker	25
JH Edrich	b Mallett	35
DS Steele	c GS Chappell b Gilmour	92
KWR Fletcher	c GS Chappell b Lillee	14
AW Greig	c & b Mallett	49
CM Old	st Marsh b Mallett	10
JH Hampshire	c GS Chappell b Thomson	0
APE Knott	c Thomson b Lillee	31
PH Edmonds	c sub (A Turner) b Gilmour	8
JA Snow	c Marsh b Gilmour	9
DL Underwood	not out	0
Extras	(b 5, lb 2, w 2, nb 9)	18
Total	(all out; 94 overs)	291

Bowling	O	M	R	W	Econ
DK Lillee	20	5	48	2	2.40
JR Thomson	20	6	67	1	3.35
GJ Gilmour	20	5	72	3	3.60
MHN Walker	15	4	36	1	2.40
AA Mallett	19	4	50	3	2.63

Fall of wickets 1-55 (Wood), 2-70 (Edrich), 3-103 (Fletcher), 4-197 (Greig), 5-209 (Old), 6-210 (Hampshire), 7-272 (Steele), 8-276 (Knott), 9-285 (Edmonds), 10-291 (Snow)

Australia 2nd innings (target: 445 runs)		RUNS
RB McCosker	not out	95
RW Marsh	b Underwood	12
IM Chappell	lbw b Old	62
GS Chappell	c Steele b Edmonds	12
KD Walters	not out	25
Extras	(b 4, lb 8, nb 2)	14
Total	(3 wickets; 73 overs)	220

Bowling	O	M	R	W	Econ
JA Snow	15	6	21	0	1.40
CM Old	17	5	61	1	3.58
AW Greig	9	3	20	0	2.22
DL Underwood	15	4	40	1	2.66
PH Edmonds	17	4	64	1	3.76

Fall of wickets 1-55 (Marsh), 2-161 (IM Chappell), 3-174 (GS Chappell)

Did not bat R Edwards, GJ Gilmour, MHN Walker, JR Thomson, DK Lillee, AA Mallett

Craig White hits the ball for four runs during the fourth Test at Melbourne on December 29, 2002. (PA)

CRAIG WHITE

Born: December 16, 1969, Morley Hall

Struck his Test century against India in the heat of Ahmedabad in December, 2001, which confirmed his significance to the England team at that time. A former captain of Yorkshire, and a Championship winner with them too, his figures underline his importance as a genuine and aggressive all-rounder: more than 12,000 first class runs and approaching 400 wickets. The sadness is that his career has been punctuated by injury, which has deprived him of greater Test recognition.

Test record:	
Span:	1994-2002
Matches:	30
Runs:	1,052
Highest score:	121
Average:	24.46
Wickets:	59
Best bowling:	5-32
Average:	37.62
Catches:	14

Melbourne:
December 26, 27, 28, 29, 30, 2002

Just occasionally, I think about the 'What ifs' in my life.

What if I'd stayed in Australia rather than coming home to Yorkshire? What if I'd played for the Aussies rather than England? What if our number ten, Andrew Caddick, hadn't tried to hit Jason Gillespie back over his head for six in the fourth Test at Melbourne? And what if I hadn't been able to 'borrow' my brother-in-law's boots before the start of the 2002-03 series in Australia?

I'll start at the beginning . . .

When I was seven years old, the family left Yorkshire for Melbourne. My grandmother was ill, and my parents essentially went to look after her. We moved into a small, gold-mining town called Bendigo about 70 miles north of the main city. I have to say that 'Poms' weren't necessarily popular or welcome. At school, one of the kids came up to me early on and said: 'My dad thinks that the only good Pom is a dead one'. I replied by giving him a smack on the jaw.

Of course, everything was geared to sport. In the winter, I played Aussie Rules. In the summer, I was obsessed with cricket. And, believe me, cricket in Australia is intensely competitive. Even a game in the street with the neighbours was played like a Test match

– nothing asked for, nothing given.

The facilities throughout the country are gold standard. Even in Bendigo, there were free outdoor nets and I could use them whenever I liked. It was there that I began to learn how to play and then develop my skills.

Slowly, I graduated through the ranks. I was in the Australian Youth Academy with figures such as Michael Slater and Michael Bevan. I went on an under-19 tour to the West Indies with Shane Warne and Damian Fleming. I was opening the batting and bowling spin. In fact, I actually bowled more overs than Warne on that tour in 1990 – 414 compared to his 329. Mind you, he took one more wicket – six to my five.

Everything changed for me when the head of the Academy, Jack Potter, who went on the 1964 Ashes tour without playing a Test, rang Bob Appleyard and recommended me to Headingley. I played a practice match, took a handful of wickets and got a half century as well. The rest is history.

I had no hesitation in accepting the chance that Yorkshire gave me – even though it meant leaving both my family and the place that had become home. In truth, my heart was always with England. In the post-Packer-World Series era, Australian cricket was undergoing its transitional phase before the emergence of such powerful teams under the captaincy of Allan Border, Mark Taylor and now Ricky Ponting.

Successful or not, it would have made no difference to me. My loyalties belonged to England and particularly my two heroes Ian Botham and David Gower. I liked the flamboyant attitude of both of them. I remember my dad took me to the Melbourne Test in 1982. I insisted on wearing my England shirt. It was the game in which Border and Jeff Thomson fell three runs short of carrying Australia to a win. Botham got Thomson out – claiming his 750th first class wicket – and Border was left unbeaten on 62. Within eight years, I was a nervous 19 year-old waiting to go into bat against Malcolm Marshall at Hampshire, and I glanced across and I saw Gower standing on the balcony at Southampton. Within another two, I was facing Botham in a County Championship match at Durham. On each occasion, I honestly thought I was going to have to pinch myself awake. I couldn't believe I was so close to the pair of them.

I had the same feeling when I made my Ashes debut at Edgbaston in 2001. After all, I still have an Australian accent. Warne got me out in the first innings for four. Gillespie claimed me in the second for nought after just six balls. We lost by an innings and I finished with figures of one for 101 (though at least it was Adam Gilchrist, who made 152).

In 2002, I was playing Grade cricket in Adelaide and staying with my sister Andrea, who is married to Darren Lehmann. The call came to join up with the England squad. Darren was away with South Australia, and I explained to Andrea that I didn't have any boots. 'Take some of Darren's,' she said. 'You'll find them in the garage'. Darren could have started a sports shop. I found about 20 pairs of distinctive, brand new Nike boots. I took two pairs with me.

We won the toss in Brisbane and unwisely put Australia in. Matthew Hayden scored 197 and Ponting got 123 in a total of 492. When I came into bat, we were five down for 270.

Darren was standing at short leg. I was taking guard and then preparing to face Glenn McGrath, who was at the top of his run. Darren glanced down at my feet and suddenly realised what I was wearing. Andrea hadn't told him about the borrowed boots. 'You've got my ******* boots on,' he said. A further barrage of expletives followed. He even yelled across to Shane Warne at slip. 'The ******** got my ******* boots on'. He told McGrath to start aiming at my toes. I really had to fight back the laugher. Here I was – facing my first ball from McGrath in an Ashes Test – and my brother-in-law was sledging me! The World Cup was coming up and Darren started insisting: 'Those are my favourite boots and I was saving them. I was going to wear them during the World Cup'. I managed to score 12 before McGrath clean bowled me.

There are two sequels to the story. When I got into the dressing room that night, Darren had left me an invoice for the boots (incidentally, I still haven't paid for them). And then in the next Test, on his home ground at Adelaide, I had him caught by Andrew Flintoff for only five. My sister refused to speak to me. I think she had this fanciful notion that I'd merely bowl half volleys that Darren could smack to the boundary for four. I got him out for the second time at Perth in the third Test – and Andrea again refused to have anything to do with me!

The highlight of my entire tour was Melbourne, which in effect is my second 'home' ground. My parents were there to see me. We were chasing a first innings total of 551 and the scoreboard had clicked around to six for 118 by the time I went in. I batted just under three hours, faced 134 balls, hit Stuart MacGill for three sixes and made 85 not out – so close to a century that would have meant so much to me. I just ran out of partners. Caddick, who came in ahead of Steve Harmison, had been batting well and sensibly. But he decided to have a dash at Gillespie and was clean bowled. 'Sorry mate,' he said afterwards 'I really thought I could hit him back over his head for six'.

What if he'd just tried to block instead?

SCORECARD

Result: Australia won by 5 wickets

Toss: Australia, who chose to bat first

Series: Australia led the 5-match series 4-0

Test debut: ML Love (Australia)

Player of the match: JL Langer (Australia)

Umpires: DL Orchard (South Africa) and RB Tiffin (Zimbabwe)

TV umpire: DB Hair

Match referee: Wasim Raja (Pakistan)

Australia 1st innings		RUNS
JL Langer	c Caddick b Dawson	250
ML Hayden	c Crawley b Caddick	102
RT Ponting	b White	21
DR Martyn	c Trescothick b White	17
SR Waugh	c Foster b White	77
ML Love	not out	62
AC Gilchrist	b Dawson	1
Extras	(lb 11, w 5, nb 5)	21
Total	(6 wickets dec; 146 overs; 588 mins)	551

Did not bat B Lee, JN Gillespie, SCG MacGill, GD McGrath

Bowling	O	M	R	W	Econ
AR Caddick	36	6	126	1	3.50
SJ Harmison	36	7	108	0	3.00
C White	33	5	133	3	4.03
RKJ Dawson	28	1	121	2	4.32
MA Butcher	13	2	52	0	4.00

Fall of wickets 1-195 (Hayden, 44.2 ov), 2-235 (Ponting, 53.5 ov), 3-265 (Martyn, 63.6 ov), 4-394 (Waugh, 103.3 ov), 5-545 (Langer, 143.5 ov), 6-551 (Gilchrist, 145.6 ov)

England 1st innings		RUNS
ME Trescothick	c Gilchrist b Lee	37
MP Vaughan	b McGrath	11
MA Butcher	lbw b Gillespie	25
N Hussain	c Hayden b MacGill	24
RKJ Dawson	c Love b MacGill	6
RWT Key	lbw b Lee	0
JP Crawley	c Langer b Gillespie	17
C White	not out	85
JS Foster	lbw b Waugh	19
AR Caddick	b Gillespie	17
SJ Harmison	c Gilchrist b Gillespie	2
Extras	(b 3, lb 10, nb 14)	27
Total	(all out; 89.3 overs; 364 mins)	270

Bowling	O	M	R	W	Econ
GD McGrath	16	5	41	1	2.56
JN Gillespie	16.3	7	25	4	1.51
SCG MacGill	36	10	108	2	3.00
B Lee	17	4	70	2	4.11
SR Waugh	4	0	13	1	3.25

Fall of wickets 1-13 (Vaughan, 6.2 ov), 2-73 (Trescothick, 22.4 ov), 3-94 (Butcher, 32.1 ov), 4-111 (Dawson, 37.6 ov), 5-113 (Key, 38.4 ov), 6-118 (Hussain, 41.6 ov), 7-172 (Crawley, 54.2 ov), 8-227 (Foster, 76.5 ov), 9-264 (Caddick, 85.5 ov), 10-270 (Harmison, 89.3 ov)

England 2nd innings (following on)		RUNS
ME Trescothick	lbw b MacGill	37
MP Vaughan	c Love b MacGill	145
MA Butcher	c Love b Gillespie	6
N Hussain	c & b McGrath	23
RWT Key	c Ponting b Gillespie	52
JP Crawley	b Lee	33
C White	c Gilchrist b MacGill	21
JS Foster	c Love b MacGill	6
RKJ Dawson	not out	15
AR Caddick	c Waugh b MacGill	10
SJ Harmison	b Gillespie	7
Extras	(b 3, lb 21, w 2, nb 6)	32
Total	(all out; 120.4 overs; 477 mins)	387

Bowling	O	M	R	W	Econ
GD McGrath	19	5	44	1	2.31
JN Gillespie	24.4	6	71	3	2.87
SCG MacGill	48	10	152	5	3.16
B Lee	27	4	87	1	3.22
SR Waugh	2	0	9	0	4.50

Fall of wickets 1-67 (Trescothick, 15.6 ov), 2-89 (Butcher, 24.6 ov), 3-169 (Hussain, 48.5 ov), 4-236 (Vaughan, 69.4 ov), 5-287 (Key, 81.1 ov), 6-342 (Crawley, 104.5 ov), 7-342 (White, 105.3 ov), 8-356 (Foster, 109.5 ov), 9-378 (Caddick, 117.5 ov), 10-387 (Harmison, 120.4 ov)

Australia 2nd innings (target: 107 runs)		RUNS
JL Langer	lbw b Caddick	24
ML Hayden	c sub (AJ Tudor) b Caddick	1
RT Ponting	c Foster b Harmison	30
DR Martyn	c Foster b Harmison	0
SR Waugh	c Butcher b Caddick	14
ML Love	not out	6
AC Gilchrist	not out	10
Extras	(b 8, lb 5, nb 9)	22
Total	(5 wickets; 23.1 overs; 113 mins)	107

Did not bat B Lee, JN Gillespie, SCG MacGill, GD McGrath

Bowling	O	M	R	W	Econ
AR Caddick	12	1	51	3	4.25
SJ Harmison	11.1	1	43	2	3.85

Fall of wickets 1-8 (Hayden, 2.1 ov), 2-58 (Ponting, 11.2 ov), 3-58 (Martyn, 11.5 ov), 4-83 (Waugh, 18.1 ov), 5-90 (Langer, 18.5 ov)

MATTHEW HOGGARD

Born: December 31, 1976, Leeds

Began his first career at Yorkshire in 1996 and made his Test debut four years later. Has so far taken almost 650 first class wickets, and 248 Test wickets. Well known for his stamina and salt-of-the-earth approach, who played 40 consecutive Tests and was at one stage ranked number four in the world. He grew up wanting to be a vet. His autobiography, Hoggy: Welcome to My World, broke new ground in its approach to a cricketer's life story and perfectly reflected the personality of the author.

Test record:

Span:	2000 – present
Matches:	67
Wickets:	248
Best bowling:	7-61
Runs:	473
Highest score:	38
Catches:	24

Trent Bridge:
August, 25, 26, 27, 28, 2005

I've always taken my batting seriously, and I try to enjoy it too. It's just as well. For goodness knows what might have happened otherwise when I came out to partner Ashley Giles at the end of the Fourth Test at Trent Bridge in that unforgettable heady summer of 2005.

We were seven wickets down, but only 13 runs from beating Australia and taking a 2-1 lead before the final Test at the Oval. I remember walking out to an almost eerie silence, as though no one in the crowd wanted to breathe in case it damaged our chances.

In the dressing room beforehand, I didn't quite know where to put myself. Every so often one of our top order would come in swearing and throw down his bat after getting out. Even though I didn't need one, I got our physio to give me a massage. It meant I didn't have to watch any more.

I don't mind admitting that I was terrified. The Ashes had become so important – not only to us but also to the country as a whole – that I didn't want to let anyone down. I knew that Ashley was terrified too. But, like it or not, the onus was on the two of us to steer England home as best we could.

But I'm getting a little ahead of myself . . .

Matthew Hoggard celebrates taking the wicket of Australia's Justin Langer during the third test in Perth in December, 2006. (PA)

We went into it firmly believing that the Ashes could be ours. We'd come so close to taking a 2-1 lead in the series in the previous Test at Old Trafford. We set them 423 to win, which was never on. We needed to take ten wickets in a day and would have done it if Ricky Ponting hadn't been so stubborn in making 156. Somehow Brett Lee and Glenn McGrath held out for the final four overs. Some people might have thought that our chance had gone. The Aussies had been down . . . and we still hadn't managed to finish them off.

But what struck me afterwards was the way in which the Aussies celebrated with a mixture of exuberance and relief. They were grateful to have escaped with a draw, which I thought said a lot about how aggressively we'd approached the Tests – no one was going to bully us with either the bat or the ball – and the way in which we'd done so much more than merely take them by surprise in the opening three Tests. We'd genuinely shaken their confidence too. The Aussies suddenly looked vulnerable, as if the prospect of losing had obviously crossed their mind more than once. I was convinced that we'd played the better cricket – and would continue that form.

That's why we went into the Trent Bridge Test with so much self-belief. And Michael Vaughan promptly won the toss, we piled up nearly 500 and then removed them for just 218. It was the first time Australia had followed on since 1988. We had one problem, however. Simon Jones wasn't completely fit, which made bowling them out again more difficult than I'd imagined. After four overs, he broke down with an ankle injury, and his workload was shared between only four of us.

We did get a helping hand from an unexpected source. Our 12th man Gary Pratt ran out Ponting for 48 with a direct hit from cover. He lost his cool and gave me a stare on the way back to the Pavilion. I asked him what he was looking at. Before he'd regained his composure, he'd ranted at Duncan Fletcher, who was sitting on the balcony. He was moaning about the use of substitute fielders because he thought our bowlers were trotting off the field for a rub down and a rest to compensate for the fact we'd lost Jones. We were actually going off for a pee because we'd taken on so much liquid to retain our levels of hydration. His reaction proved one thing to me. We'd really got them rattled.

When the last wicket went down, Australia were on 387. We needed 129 to win, which looked straightforward to me. I should have known better.

Whatever score we're chasing – even when it's a low one – I always think that I might have to bat at some stage, and so I prepare for it. If I don't, and I'm suddenly caught rushing around for my pads, I won't be mentally ready to go out into the middle. At Test level, there's always the chance you'll have to go in. Players have more time to prepare for a Test than a County Championship match. You have a proper net, which means you can bowl a lot of overs as well as face them too. I think it has helped my batting over the years.

The Aussies had lost McGrath before the Test began with a damaged elbow. Shaun Tait came in for his Test debut. But we still had to contend with Brett Lee and Shane Warne. One of them was hurtling the ball down at 95mph-plus, and the other was turning it a yard. Apart from that, we didn't have much to worry about!

We lost second innings wickets through some superb bowling and a few indiscreet shots (Geraint Jones holed out after trying to lift Warne over the Pavilion). The longer things went on, the more tense things became. I wasn't surprised. I'd always had the suspicion that the match would have more twists and turns before it ended. I think this pragmatic approach helped me.

When Lee clean bowled Andrew Flintoff, I knew my moment had almost come. Once I was out in the middle, my nerves vanished and I actually felt fairly confident. I just focussed on the job. But then I much prefer being out there to going through the sitting in the dressing room watching someone else. Your destiny is in your own hands.

Even at his extreme pace, the good thing about Lee is that he gives you a sight of the ball. You can follow his arm, which is high and stylish and doesn't particularly alter from one delivery to the next. It can be difficult to sight Fidel Edwards or Shoaib Akhtar - and especially Lasith Malinga – because their action can change. Lee's doesn't – or at least not as noticeably.

I suppose I got lucky too. It isn't every day that Lee bowls you a full toss wide on off stump. When it left his hand, I knew I'd got to go for it. The ball hit the middle of the bat and flew through extra cover – though, in hindsight, I think the crowd's intake of breath actually sucked it to the boundary.

Our win meant that we went to the Oval as favourites. It is usually easy for me to switch off. I don't read newspapers very often, and I don't necessarily follow the news either. To relax, I just go home and close the door behind me. When I opened it again, it was usually to take my two dogs (now I've got three) across the moors for a walk. There's no better way to put things into perspective. But this Ashes series followed me and the rest of the team everywhere. It was impossible to ignore all the coverage. I remember the last day of the Test at Old Trafford, where the crowds were so huge that it took us almost an hour to go from the hotel to the ground, which was normally just a 15 minute ride. It was the proof – if we needed it – of how much the public cared about the series. When 20,000 people get locked out of a cricket match, you know it's something special.

I'm not one of those bowlers who sits down and goes through a painstaking analysis of everything. We watched videos as a team and people came up with various ideas and I'm sure that Duncan Fletcher knew before the start of that series where he wanted us to bowl to every Australian batsman. My view remains simply this: If you get it on the good length and make it go away or jag in, it's going to cause a batsman problems whoever he is and however many runs he's scored. That's the attitude and strategy I always employ. It got my first wicket of the series. I clean bowled Matthew Hayden through the gate at Lord's, and shouted my lungs out in a release of tension that had been building for weeks.

I say this to emphasise that I think I'm a practical, down to earth guy who doesn't get carried away. But I have to say that I was unbelievably nervous on the first morning at the Oval. It was far worse than preparing to bat at Trent Bridge. And on the last morning – when Kevin Pietersen was spraying shots to all parts of the ground – I was even worse. I dragged Ashley Giles off to play cards. I couldn't watch what was happening. We sat in the coach's room at the back of the dressing room.

To win the Ashes fulfilled a lifetime ambition for me. In the year preceding the series, we'd done our best not to talk about it. When it was mentioned, we tried to remind ourselves that we'd got other Test matches to win before we faced Australia. All the same, we knew – irrespective of our previous results – that we'd be judged as a team on whether we'd won or lost the Ashes. We set ourselves targets and ticked all the boxes. We were aggressive. We didn't allow the Australians to push us around. We weren't saying 'hello mate' to them all the time.

I took 16 wickets in the series and felt I'd played my part. Most of all, I'll never forget the day after we won at The Oval. To say the least, we'd enjoyed ourselves the night before. It was one heck of a party. But when someone mentioned that we'd be going on an open topped bus tour, I honestly thought two men and a dog would turn up. I suppose I'd forgotten that cricket, however briefly, had caught hold of the national imagination. To be on the top deck and stare around at the crowds and the flags and banners – and to hear the chanting and shouting – will stay with me forever.

The real significance of the Ashes week came to me a week or so later. I'd called at a drive-in Burger King. As I went to pay, the staff said: 'You won the Ashes – the least we can do is give you a free meal'. Now that's sporting success for you!

SCORECARD

Result: England won by 3 wickets

Toss: England, who chose to bat first

Series: England led the 5-match series 2-1

Test debut: SW Tait (Australia)

Player of the match: A Flintoff (England)

Umpires: Aleem Dar (Pakistan) and SA Bucknor (West Indies)

TV umpire: MR Benson

Match referee: RS Madugalle (Sri Lanka)

England 1st innings		RUNS
ME Trescothick	b Tait	65
AJ Strauss	c Hayden b Warne	35
MP Vaughan	c Gilchrist b Ponting	58
IR Bell	c Gilchrist b Tait	3
KP Pietersen	c Gilchrist b Lee	45
A Flintoff	lbw b Tait	102
GO Jones	c & b Kasprowicz	85
AF Giles	lbw b Warne	15
MJ Hoggard	c Gilchrist b Warne	10
SJ Harmison	st Gilchrist b Warne	2
SP Jones	not out	15
Extras	(b 1, lb 15, w 1, nb 25)	42
Total	(all out; 123.1 overs; 537 mins)	477

Bowling	O	M	R	W	Econ
B Lee	32	2	131	1	4.09
MS Kasprowicz	32	3	122	1	3.81
SW Tait	24	4	97	3	4.04
SK Warne	29.1	4	102	4	3.49
RT Ponting	6	2	9	1	1.50

Fall of wickets 1-105 (Strauss, 21.4 ov), 2-137 (Trescothick, 30.5 ov), 3-146 (Bell, 34.1 ov), 4-213 (Vaughan, 55.2 ov), 5-241 (Pietersen, 64.1 ov), 6-418 (Flintoff, 103.2 ov), 7-450 (GO Jones, 112.5 ov), 8-450 (Giles, 113.1 ov), 9-454 (Harmison, 115.1 ov), 10-477 (Hoggard, 123.1 ov)

Australia 1st innings		RUNS
JL Langer	c Bell b Hoggard	27
ML Hayden	lbw b Hoggard	7
RT Ponting	lbw b SP Jones	1
DR Martyn	lbw b Hoggard	1
MJ Clarke	lbw b Harmison	36
SM Katich	c Strauss b SP Jones	45
AC Gilchrist	c Strauss b Flintoff	27
SK Warne	c Bell b SP Jones	0
B Lee	c Bell b SP Jones	47
MS Kasprowicz	b SP Jones	5
SW Tait	not out	3
Extras	(lb 2, w 1, nb 16)	19
Total	(all out; 49.1 overs; 247 mins)	218

Bowling	O	M	R	W	Econ
SJ Harmison	9	1	48	1	5.33
MJ Hoggard	15	3	70	3	4.66
SP Jones	14.1	4	44	5	3.10
A Flintoff	11	1	54	1	4.90

Fall of wickets 1-20 (Hayden, 9.3 ov), 2-21 (Ponting, 10.3 ov), 3-22 (Martyn, 11.1 ov), 4-58 (Langer, 19.3 ov), 5-99 (Clarke, 30.3 ov), 6-157 (Katich, 39.2 ov), 7-157 (Warne, 39.3 ov), 8-163 (Gilchrist, 42.2 ov), 9-175 (Kasprowicz, 43.2 ov), 10-218 (Lee, 49.1 ov)

Australia 2nd innings (following on)		RUNS
JL Langer	c Bell b Giles	61
ML Hayden	c Giles b Flintoff	26
RT Ponting	run out (sub [GJ Pratt])	48
DR Martyn	c GO Jones b Flintoff	13
MJ Clarke	c GO Jones b Hoggard	56
SM Katich	lbw b Harmison	59
AC Gilchrist	lbw b Hoggard	11
SK Warne	st GO Jones b Giles	45
B Lee	not out	26
MS Kasprowicz	c GO Jones b Harmison	19
SW Tait	b Harmison	4
Extras	(b 1, lb 4, nb 14)	19
Total	(all out; 124 overs; 548 mins)	387

Bowling	O	M	R	W	Econ
MJ Hoggard	27	7	72	2	2.66
SP Jones	4	0	15	0	3.75
SJ Harmison	30	5	93	3	3.10
A Flintoff	29	4	83	2	2.86
AF Giles	28	3	107	2	3.82
IR Bell	6	2	12	0	2.00

Fall of wickets 1-50 (Hayden, 13.4 ov), 2-129 (Langer, 33.6 ov), 3-155 (Ponting, 44.1 ov), 4-161 (Martyn, 46.1 ov), 5-261 (Clarke, 94.2 ov), 6-277 (Gilchrist, 98.5 ov), 7-314 (Katich, 107.3 ov), 8-342 (Warne, 112.3 ov), 9-373 (Kasprowicz, 119.2 ov), 10-387 (Tait, 123.6 ov)

England 2nd innings (target: 129 runs)		RUNS
ME Trescothick	c Ponting b Warne	27
AJ Strauss	c Clarke b Warne	23
MP Vaughan	c Hayden b Warne	0
IR Bell	c Kasprowicz b Lee	3
KP Pietersen	c Gilchrist b Lee	23
A Flintoff	b Lee	26
GO Jones	c Kasprowicz b Warne	3
AF Giles	not out	7
MJ Hoggard	not out	8
Extras	(lb 4, nb 5)	9
Total	(7 wickets; 31.5 overs; 168 mins)	129

Bowling	O	M	R	W	Econ
B Lee	12	0	51	3	4.25
MS Kasprowicz	2	0	19	0	9.50
SK Warne	13.5	2	31	4	2.24
SW Tait	4	0	24	0	6.00

Fall of wickets 1-32 (Trescothick, 5.1 ov), 2-36 (Vaughan, 7.1 ov), 3-57 (Strauss, 13.5 ov), 4-57 (Bell, 14.1 ov), 5-103 (Pietersen, 24.1 ov), 6-111 (Flintoff, 26.4 ov), 7-116 (GO Jones, 27.6 ov)

Did not bat SJ Harmison, SP Jones

MICHAEL VAUGHAN

Born: October 29, 1974, Eccles

As captain of the Ashes winning team of 2005, he secured his place among England's sporting immortals. He began his Test career in Johannesburg when England were already four wickets down with only two runs on the board. He went on to make 33 of 84 balls and in the process revealed the calm, unhurried temperament that characterised so much of his captaincy.

Test record:	
Span:	1999-present
Matches:	82
Runs:	5,719
Highest score:	197
Catches:	44
Wickets:	6
Best bowling:	2-71

Edgbaston:
August 4, 5, 6, 7, 2005.

Every game in this amazing Ashes series was remarkable in its own right and put together they formed one of the greatest rubbers of all time between England and Australia.

The scenes which followed on from regaining the Ashes at The Oval will remain imprinted in the minds all of the England players who took part for the rest of our lives but it is worth recalling that we actually lost the first Test at Lord's by the wide margin of 239 runs. Despite the heavy defeat, I still took a lot of positives from the game because we got 20 wickets and the atmosphere on that first morning was electric. Australia won the toss and batted but we got at them very, very hard and bowled them out for 190 with Steve Harmison picking up five of the wickets. Glenn McGrath and Shane Warne bowled superbly to send us back for 155 and put Australia on top but at the end of the match I was encouraged by the fact that none of the Aussie batsmen had managed a century while Harmison, Freddie Flintoff, Simon Jones and Matthew Hoggard had looked like they had the makings of getting 20 wickets consistently. I always think if you get 20 wickets you have a great chance of winning a Test match.

The big thing was how we went about coping with going 1-0 down when the media and the public obviously thought that was the end of the road and had written us off. I thought we just needed to get to Edgbaston and try to play positively and aggressively and do everything we had talked about. I think the first day at Edgbaston was a crucial day in the context of the whole series. We were 1-0 down; McGrath got injured in the warm-ups and was out of the match; we lost the toss and were put in but we still managed to smash 407 in 80 overs in the day and so set up a thrilling game of cricket that had everything. You can't really dream up a fabulous Test match like this one, which we went on to win by two runs, but for it to occur against Australia in a series which had been built up so big was very, very special. We produced entertaining, attacking, ballsy cricket and had a real go at the Aussies in very much their own style of things. It was a brilliant game of cricket. On the second day we bowled them out for 182 and got a decent lead. Then magician Warne produced two or three gems and Brett Lee bowled fast.

We looked like we were only going to set them 190-200 but Simon Jones and Freddie then produced this great last wicket partnership which put on 51. That stand swayed the momentum towards England and we went on to the field determined to get ten wickets. Justin Langer and Matthew Hayden put on a few for the first wicket but Freddie then produced what must be one of the best overs you will see in Test cricket in a long, long time. He gets Langer out with one which nips back and bowls him and then he produces three gems to Rickie Ponting…. in, in and then he does him with an away-swinger to have him caught behind. Everything from that point seemed to go our way and every move we made was a good one. The ball was reverse swinging and we took the extra half hour and for a time we probably thought we were going to win the game on the Saturday evening. In the event, Harmy captured the eighth wicket in the last over with a slower ball which deceived Michael Clarke and that was a huge bonus. The ball was still reverse swinging and I must admit I went to bed on Saturday night thinking 'Crickey, surely on Sunday morning ten or 15 minutes are all we'll need to be 1-1 in the series'. But I never envisaged Warnie slashing it and Lee showing all that fight and determination and Kasprowicz also playing well, so it became a real nipper.

It was funny because the nearer they got to winning the more I could sense they were starting to think about the situation whereas before that they had just been swinging and having a really good dash. This gave me a little bit of optimism because when you get tail-enders thinking like that you have more of a chance. We got a great opportunity to end it when Kasprowicz steered Freddie to third man but Simon didn't hold on to it. We just tried to make the game go on as long as we could and I put men on the edge to try to stop Lee and Kasprowicz getting boundaries and ending it quickly. Then came that over when Harmie bowled a full bunger to Lee who smashed it straight to deep cover and probably four or five yards either side would have been the end of the game. The next ball he bounces Kasprowicz, it takes the glove and Geraint Jones holds a fantastic catch behind the stumps. We had just won one of the greatest Test matches ever played and there was a real feel among the side from that moment on that we could regain the Ashes.

The drawn Test at Old Trafford was the one in which I felt we played our most consistent cricket of the whole series. There was only one period on the Saturday - when Warne got hold of us a bit with the bat - that we weren't in control of the game. For the most part, we were very much in charge and we played very aggressively. We won a very good toss, got a decent score on the board and the ball started to reverse swing. We set a hard target on that fourth evening and on the Monday there were 20-odd thousand locked out of the ground and the roads clogged with traffic. It really hit home to us that this Ashes series was capturing a lot of imaginations and that we had all the country right behind us. We were left one wicket shy of what would have been an incredible victory. We saw the Aussies actually celebrating a draw which was something we had not seen for many, many years. So I took great heart from seeing so many legends in their team celebrating on the balcony for drawing a game with us! I believed that if we continued doing the things we were doing and continued to attack then we would get our rewards by the end of the series. Although my own contribution to the match was pretty special – 166 in the first innings – I have to say that I had felt in good nick before that. I played poorly at Lord's but even though I only got 24 first dig at Edgbaston I sensed that a big score was just around the corner. Again, it was a good toss to win and I batted well and very aggressively, attacking their bowlers and taking them on. I had a little bit of luck, bowled off a no-ball and dropped, but you warrant that luck when you do a lot of hard work and I was delighted to get a good score on the board.

Trent Bridge was another good win but it was a lot closer than we all wanted. It was yet another good toss to win and it meant we had batted first in all four Tests so far. We got runs on the board and I think you can dictate the game if you do that. The ball was swinging around as it always does at Trent Bridge and we love playing there because of that reason. The crowds were really patriotic and behind us. Some of the guys put in some great individual performances but I thought the most important thing was that we held some terrific catches. I particularly remember Andrew Strauss in the first innings getting Gilchrist out. Freddie produced a great delivery and Gilchrist 'snook' it and Strauss stuck his hand out flying through the air at second slip. Those are the sort of moments which help to win a series. When you look back at it all and wonder why you won, it is these little moments of brilliance in the field or one or two special deliveries or the guy who goes on from 100 to 170 or 180…these are the things that get you the Ashes.

Finally, The Oval and the last part of our epic adventure. Yet again, I won a good toss which was great but I don't think we were up to par in the first innings, despite Strauss' terrific 129. I felt our 373 was still probably 60 or 70 runs short of where we should have been. Langer and Hayden had a first wicket partnership of 185, then there was a lot of weather around and a lot of bad light. We were off for light on a few occasions and we seemed to hang around for a long time until Sunday and then Freddie and Hoggy produced two splendid spells. We bowled them out about level and we knew then that we had to bat for near on a day to win the Ashes. Sometimes it is difficult to bat in that situation because you have everything to lose if you fail but we were saved by Kevin Pietersen's extraordinary innings. The crowds throughout the series were incredible but on that last day there was an eeriness about the whole arena and the whole of The Oval. It was a very special atmosphere and something I will always remember.

SCORECARD

Result: England won by 2 runs

Toss: Australia, who chose to field first

Series: 5-match series level 1-1

Player of the match: A Flintoff (England)

Umpires: BF Bowden (New Zealand) and RE Koertzen (South Africa)

TV umpire: JW Lloyds

Match referee: RS Madugalle (Sri Lanka)

England 1st innings		RUNS
ME Trescothick	c †Gilchrist b Kasprowicz	90
AJ Strauss	b Warne	48
MP Vaughan	c Lee b Gillespie	24
IR Bell	c †Gilchrist b Kasprowicz	6
KP Pietersen	c Katich b Lee	71
A Flintoff	c †Gilchrist b Gillespie	68
GO Jones	c †Gilchrist b Kasprowicz	1
AF Giles	lbw b Warne	23
MJ Hoggard	lbw b Warne	16
SJ Harmison	b Warne	17
SP Jones	not out	19
Extras	(lb 9, w 1, nb 14)	24
Total	(all out; 79.2 overs; 356 mins)	407

Bowling	O	M	R	W	Econ
B Lee	17	1	111	1	6.52
JN Gillespie	22	3	91	2	4.13
MS Kasprowicz	15	3	80	3	5.33
SK Warne	25.2	4	116	4	4.57

Fall of wickets 1-112 (Strauss, 25.3 ov), 2-164 (Trescothick, 32.3 ov), 3-170 (Bell, 32.6 ov), 4-187 (Vaughan, 36.6 ov), 5-290 (Flintoff, 54.3 ov), 6-293 (GO Jones, 57.4 ov), 7-342 (Giles, 65.1 ov), 8-348 (Pietersen, 66.3 ov), 9-375 (Harmison, 69.4 ov), 10-407 (Hoggard, 79.2 ov)

Australia 1st innings		RUNS
JL Langer	lbw b SP Jones	82
ML Hayden	c Strauss b Hoggard	0
RT Ponting	c Vaughan b Giles	61
DR Martyn	run out (Vaughan)	20
MJ Clarke	c †GO Jones b Giles	40
SM Katich	c †GO Jones b Flintoff	4
AC Gilchrist	not out	49
SK Warne	b Giles	8
B Lee	c Flintoff b SP Jones	6
JN Gillespie	lbw b Flintoff	7
MS Kasprowicz	lbw b Flintoff	0
Extras	(b 13, lb 7, w 1, nb 10)	31
Total	(all out; 76 overs; 346 mins)	308

Bowling	O	M	R	W	Econ
SJ Harmison	11	1	48	0	4.36
MJ Hoggard	8	0	41	1	5.12
SP Jones	16	2	69	2	4.31
A Flintoff	15	1	52	3	3.46
AF Giles	26	2	78	3	3.00

Fall of wickets 1-0 (Hayden, 1.1 ov), 2-88 (Ponting, 19.5 ov), 3-118 (Martyn, 24.5 ov), 4-194 (Clarke, 44.2 ov), 5-208 (Katich, 49.4 ov), 6-262 (Langer, 61.3 ov), 7-273 (Warne, 64.5 ov), 8-282 (Lee, 67.1 ov), 9-308 (Gillespie, 75.5 ov), 10-308 (Kasprowicz, 75.6 ov)

England 2nd innings		RUNS
ME Trescothick	c †Gilchrist b Lee	21
AJ Strauss	b Warne	6
MJ Hoggard	c Hayden b Lee	1
MP Vaughan	b Lee	1
IR Bell	c †Gilchrist b Warne	21
KP Pietersen	c †Gilchrist b Warne	20
A Flintoff	b Warne	73
GO Jones†	c Ponting b Lee	9
AF Giles	c Hayden b Warne	8
SJ Harmison	c Ponting b Warne	0
SP Jones	not out	12
Extras	(lb 1, nb 9)	10
Total	(all out; 52.1 overs; 249 mins)	182

Bowling	O	M	R	W	Econ
B Lee	18	1	82	4	4.55
JN Gillespie	8	0	24	0	3.00
MS Kasprowicz	3	0	29	0	9.66
SK Warne	23.1	7	46	6	1.98

Fall of wickets 1-25 (Strauss, 6.2 ov), 2-27 (Trescothick, 11.2 ov), 3-29 (Vaughan, 11.5 ov), 4-31 (Hoggard, 13.5 ov), 5-72 (Pietersen, 24.6 ov), 6-75 (Bell, 26.5 ov), 7-101 (GO Jones, 33.6 ov), 8-131 (Giles, 44.3 ov), 9-131 (Harmison, 44.4 ov), 10-182 (Flintoff, 52.1 ov)

Australia 2nd innings (target: 282 runs)		RUNS
JL Langer	b Flintoff	28
ML Hayden	c Trescothick b SP Jones	31
RT Ponting	c †GO Jones b Flintoff	0
DR Martyn	c Bell b Hoggard	28
MJ Clarke	b Harmison	30
SM Katich	c Trescothick b Giles	16
AC Gilchrist	c Flintoff b Giles	1
JN Gillespie	lbw b Flintoff	0
SK Warne	hit wicket b Flintoff	42
B Lee	not out	43
MS Kasprowicz	c †GO Jones b Harmison	20
Extras	(b 13, lb 8, w 1, nb 18)	40
Total	(all out; 64.3 overs; 307 mins)	279

Bowling	O	M	R	W	Econ
SJ Harmison	17.3	3	62	2	3.54
MJ Hoggard	5	0	26	1	5.20
AF Giles	15	3	68	2	4.53
A Flintoff	22	3	79	4	3.59
SP Jones	5	1	23	1	4.60

Fall of wickets 1-47 (Langer, 12.2 ov), 2-48 (Ponting, 12.6 ov), 3-82 (Hayden, 22.5 ov), 4-107 (Martyn, 26.1 ov), 5-134 (Katich, 31.6 ov), 6-136 (Gilchrist, 33.5 ov), 7-137 (Gillespie, 34.2 ov), 8-175 (Clarke, 43.4 ov), 9-220 (Warne, 52.1 ov), 10-279 (Kasprowicz, 64.3 ov)

Michael Vaughan. (PA)

AFTERWORD

TONY GREIG

In my day – and I'm sure it's still the case now – the England team always relished the Headingley Test. There were a lot of reasons for this.

For starters, we received the level of support that Yorkshiremen usually reserved for their own. We felt as though it was emphatically a 'home' ground for us. I'm not saying that we didn't get backing from crowds elsewhere, such as Trent Bridge or The Oval. But the degree of the partisanship at Headingley was greater in my view – this was a good feeling and it gave us a significant advantage because our opposition were aware of it too.

I also thought of the Yorkshire crowd as both knowledgeable and profoundly passionate about the game. In the 1970s, I think it stemmed – as it did across the border in Lancashire – from the tradition of hard League cricket as much as the rich history of the county team itself. I found it was the same whenever I played there for Sussex too. Headingley had a soul, which stretched back to the era of Hirst and Rhodes.

Most importantly, Headingley and the Yorkshire climate nearly always provided us with what are best described as 'typical English' conditions. Playing for Sussex at Hove, I didn't see too many mornings or afternoons of low, brooding cloud. On overcast days at Headingley, the cloud cover signalled one thing – a lot of swing and seam. There was nearly always movement in the air and off the pitch, and our bowlers were able to exploit this better than the tourists. The English ball has a seam that protrudes more than the Kookaburra, which was used elsewhere. Combined with the grey skies, it made lively, eventful and interesting cricket. If we needed a wicket or two, Alan Knott and I often glanced at the clouds and willed them towards the ground.

I have to admit that my most memorable Headingley experience wasn't against the Australians. It came in the 'Grovel' series with the West Indies in 1976. My use of the word 'grovel' obscures almost everything else we did during that summer. In the fourth Test at Headingley, I scored 116 in the first innings and 76 not out in the second. We only lost by 55 runs partially because I ran out of partners. Whenever I'm captured on TV during the Windies 'blackwash', the clip of film is always the same: the one where Michael Holding demolishes my stumps at The Oval!

Two Headingley Ashes Tests are still prominent in my memory. In 1972, there'd been a thunderstorm over the weekend before the match, which meant the groundsman couldn't use the heavy roller. The Australians were raging that a fungus called fusarium which causes root rot had left the strip bare. The Aussies spent so much time whinging about the state of the surface that I think it affected their game. The truth is Derek Underwood was just devastating. He was far too good for the Aussie batsmen – and he turned the ball a foot. He finished with match figures of 10 for 82 and we won by nine wickets with two days and almost two hours to spare. His performance retained the Ashes for us.

In 1975 – after I'd taken over from Mike Denness and become England captain – we were on the verge of beating Australia when I came down for breakfast on the final day. The chairman of selectors, Alec Bedser, came over with a grim face and said: 'We need to get to the ground'. The pitch had been vandalised by protesters campaigning for the release of a convicted criminal, who none of us had heard of. The surface was cut up and smeared with a gallon of oil. I remember inspecting the damage with the Australian captain Ian Chappell. We talked briefly about finding another part of the square on which to cut a new pitch. I didn't think it was right to expect the Australians, who were 220-3 and chasing more than 400 to win, to bat on a different pitch. Ian was slightly taken aback that I was prepared to be scrupulously fair to them. I wanted to win – but not like that. It would have been a hollow victory.

I always admired the Yorkshire teams even if there was squabbling between them off the field, the pull-together, competitive edge remained on it. I think two players embodied this most of all for me: Ray Illingworth and Geoff Boycott.

Illy was the mastermind in our 1972 England side and the best captain I ever played with or against. He was a tough man, a wonderful strategic thinker and a first-rate tactician. I respected him enormously. There was never any fuss or histrionics in team meetings or in the dressing room. He got on with the job in a firm, but unflustered way. There was stiff competition for the captaincy during this period. The cricket 'establishment' was inclined to push Colin Cowdrey's claims, and I believe Illy felt that one bad run would give them an excuse to make the change. I think this explains why he didn't bowl himself more in Tests. He'd won the Ashes Down Under in 1970-71, and then made sure of clinging on to them that day at Headingley. He became one of England's most successful skippers and proved a point as well.

I won a Test with Boycs in Trinidad on Denness' tour of the West Indies in 1973. He scored more than 200 runs and I finished with 13 wickets. In the County Championship, John Snow used to measure himself against how well he bowled to two batsmen – Boycs and Barry Richards. These were like mini-Tests to him.

I can give no higher praise to Boycs than this: I just wish he hadn't decided to opt for self-imposed exile from Tests for so long in the early to mid-70s. Every time I went to an England selection meeting, I'd always ask the same question: 'Is Boycott available?'

I always hoped I'd be told: 'Yes, he is'.

RECORDS SECTION

PLAYERS TEST RECORDS

BOB APPLEYARD

June, 1954: 5-51/2-72 v Pakistan, Trent Bridge (England won by an innings and 129 runs)

December, 1954: 8 + 19*; 0-32/1-12 v Australia, Sydney (England won by 38 runs)

December, 1954: 1* + 6; 2-38/1-17 v Australia, Melbourne (England won by 128 runs)

January, 1955: 10*; 3-58/3-13 v Australia, Adelaide (England won by five wickets)

February, 1955: 1-54 v Australia, Sydney (Match drawn)

March, 1955: 0*; 0-16/2-19 v New Zealand, Dunedin (England won by eight wickets)

March, 1955: 6; 3-38/7-4 v New Zealand, Auckland (England won by an innings and 20 runs)

June, 1955: 0*; 2-46/0-32 v South Africa, Trent Bridge (England won by an innings and five runs)

June, 1956: 1*; 2-17/0-32 v Australia, Trent Bridge (Match drawn)

BILL ATHEY

August, 1980: 9 + 1 v Australia, Lord's (Match drawn)

March, 1981: 2 + 1 v West Indies, Antigua (Match drawn)

April, 1981: 3 + 1 v West Indies, Jamaica (Match drawn)

June, 1981: 32 + 8 v India, Headingley (India won by 279 runs)

July, 1981: 0 + 38 v India, Edgbaston (Match drawn)

July, 1986: 44 + 16 v New Zealand, Lord's (Match drawn)

August, 1986: 55 + 6 v New Zealand, Trent Bridge (New Zealand won by eight wickets)

August, 1986: 17 v New Zealand, The Oval (Match drawn)

November, 1986: 76 + 1 v Australia, Brisbane (England won by seven wickets)

November, 1986: 96 + 6 v Australia, Perth (Match drawn)

November, 1986: 21 v Australia, Melbourne (England won by an innings and 14 runs)

December, 1986: 55 + 12 v Australia, Adelaide (Match drawn)

January, 1987: 5 + 31 v Australia, Sydney (Australia won by 55 runs)

June, 1987: 19 v Pakistan, Old Trafford (Match drawn)

June, 1987: 123 v Pakistan, Lord's (Match drawn)

July, 1987: 4 + 26 v Pakistan, Headingley (Pakistan won by an innings and 18 runs)

July, 1987: 0 + 14* v Pakistan, Edgbaston (Match drawn)

November, 1987: 5 + 2 v Pakistan, Lahore (Pakistan won by an innings and 87 runs)

December, 1987: 27 + 20 v Pakistan, Faisalabad (Match drawn)

December, 1987: 26 + 12 v Pakistan, Karachi (Match drawn)

January, 1988: 37 v Australia, Sydney, Bicentenary Test (Match drawn)

February, 1988: 22 + 19 v New Zealand, Christchurch (Match drawn)

July, 1989: 16 + 11 v West Indies, Headingley (West Indies won by ten wickets)

GEOFF BOYCOTT

June, 1964: 48 v Australia, Trent Bridge (Match drawn)

July, 1964: 38 + 4 v Australia, Headingley (Australia won by seven wickets)

July, 1964: 58; 0-3 v Australia, Old Trafford (Match drawn)

August, 1964: 30+113 v Australia, The Oval (Match drawn)

December, 1964: 73 v South Africa, Durban (England won by an innings and 104 runs)

December, 1964: 4 v South Africa, Johannesburg (Match drawn)

January, 1965: 15 + 1*; 3-47 v South Africa, Cape Town (Match drawn)

January, 1965: 5 + 76*; 0-25 v South Africa, Johannesburg (Mach drawn)

February, 1965: 117 + 7; 1-69/1-13 v South Africa, Port Elizabeth (Match drawn)

May, 1965: 23 + 44* v New Zealand, Edgbaston (England won by nine wickets)

June, 1965: 14 + 76 v New Zealand, Lord's (England won by seven wickets)

July, 1965: 31 + 28 v South Africa, Lord's (Match drawn)

August, 1965: 0 + 16; 0-60 v South Africa, Trent Bridge (South Africa won by 94 runs)

December, 1965: 45 + 63*; 0-16 v Australia, Brisbane (Match drawn)

December, 1965: 51 + 5*; 2-32 v Australia, Melbourne (Match drawn)

January, 1966: 84; 0-8 v Australia, Sydney (England won by an innings and 93 runs)

January, 1966: 22 + 12; 0-33 v Australia, Adelaide (Australia won by an innings and nine runs)

February, 1966: 17 + 1 v Australia, Melbourne (Match drawn)

February, 1966: 4 + 4; 0-30 v New Zealand, Christchurch (Match drawn)

March, 1966: 5 v New Zealand, Dunedin (Match drawn)

June, 1966: 60 + 25 v West Indies, Lord's (Match drawn)

June, 1966: 0 + 71 v West Indies, Trent Bridge (West Indies won by 139 runs)

August, 1966: 12 + 14 v West Indies, Headingley (West Indies won by an innings and 55 runs)

August, 1966: 4 v West Indies, The Oval (England won by an innings and 34 runs)

June, 1967: 246* v India,

Headingley (England won by six wickets)

July, 1967: 25 + 6 v India, Edgbaston (England won by 132 runs)

August, 1967: 15 + 1* v Pakistan, Trent Bridge (England won by 10 wickets)

January, 1968: 68 v West Indies, Port of Spain (Match drawn)

February, 1968: 17 + 0 v West Indies, Kingston (Match drawn)

February, 1968: 90 v West Indies, Bridgetown (Match drawn)

March, 1968: 62 + 80* v West Indies, Port of Spain (England won by seven wickets)

March, 1968: 116 + 30 v West Indies, Georgetown (Match drawn)

June, 1968: 35 + 11 v Australia, Old Trafford (Australia won by 159 runs)

June, 1968: 49 v Australia, Lord's (Match drawn)

July, 1968: 36 + 31 v Australia, Edgbaston (Match drawn)

June, 1969: 128 + 1* v West Indies, Old Trafford (England won by 10 wickets)

June, 1969: 23 + 106 v West Indies, Lord's (Match drawn)

July, 1969: 12 + 0 v West Indies, Headingley (England won by 30 runs)

July, 1969: 0 + 47 v New Zealand, Lord's (England won by 230 runs)

August, 1969: 0 v New Zealand, Trent Bridge (Match drawn)

August, 1969: 46 + 8 v New Zealand, The Oval (England won by eight wickets)

November, 1970: 37 + 16 v Australia, Brisbane (Match drawn)

December, 1970: 70 + 50 v Australia, Perth (Match drawn)

January, 1971: 77 + 120* v Australia, Sydney (England won by 299 runs)

January, 1971: 12 + 76* v Australia, Melbourne (Match drawn)

January, 1971: 58 + 119* v Australia, Adelaide (Match drawn)

June, 1971: 121* v Pakistan, Lord's (Match drawn)

July, 1971: 112 + 13 v Pakistan, Headingley (England won by 25 runs)

July, 1971: 3 + 33 v India, Lord's

(Match drawn)

June, 1972: 8 + 47 v Australia, Old Trafford (England won by 89 runs)

June, 1972: 11 + 6 v Australia, Lord's (Australia won by eight wickets)

June, 1973: 51 + 1 v New Zealand, Trent Bridge (England won by 38 runs)

June, 1973: 61 + 92 v New Zealand, Lord's (Match drawn)

July, 1973: 115 v New Zealand, Headingley (England won by an innings and one run)

July, 1973: 97 + 30 v West Indies, The Oval (West Indies won by an innings and 158 runs)

August, 1973: 56* v West Indies, Edgbaston (Match drawn)

August, 1973: 4 + 15 v West Indies, Lord's (West Indies won by an innings and 226 runs)

February, 1974: 6 + 93 v West Indies, Port of Spain (West Indies won by seven wickets)

February, 1974: 68 + 5 v West Indies, Kingston (Match drawn)

March, 1974: 10 + 13 v West Indies, Bridgetown (Match drawn)

March, 1974: 15 v West Indies, Georgetown (Match drawn)

March, 1974: 99 + 112 v West Indies, Port of Spain (England won by 26 runs)

June, 1974: 10 + 6 v India, Old Trafford (England won by 113 runs)

June, 1977: 107 + 80* v Australia, Trent Bridge (England won by seven wickets)

August, 1977: 191 v Australia, Headingley (England won by an innings and 85 runs)

August, 1977: 39 + 25* v Australia, The Oval (Match drawn)

December, 1977: 63; 0-14 v Pakistan, Lahore (Match drawn)

January, 1978: 79 + 100* v Pakistan, Hyderabad (Match drawn)

January, 1978: 31 + 56 v Pakistan, Karachi (Match drawn)

February, 1978: 77 + 1 v New Zealand, Wellington (New Zealand won by 72 runs)

February, 1978: 8 + 26 v New Zealand, Christchurch (England won by 174 runs)

March, 1978: 54 v New Zealand, Auckland (Match drawn)

August, 1978: 131 v New Zealand, Trent Bridge (England won by an innings and 119 runs)

August, 1978: 24 + 4 v New Zealand, Lord's (England won by seven wickets)

December, 1978: 13 + 16 v Australia, Brisbane (England won by seven wickets)

December, 1978: 77 + 23 v Australia, Perth (England won by 166 runs)

December, 1978: 1 + 38 v Australia, Melbourne (Australia won by 103 runs)

January, 1979: 8 + 0 v Australia, Sydney (England won by 93 runs)

January, 1979: 6 + 49 v Australia, Adelaide (England won by 205 runs)

February, 1979: 19 + 13; 0-6 v Australia, Sydney (England won by nine wickets)

July, 1979: 155; 0-8 v India, Edgbaston (England won by an innings and 83 runs)

August, 1979: 32 v India, Lord's (Match drawn)

August, 1979: 31; 0-0 v India, Headingley (Match drawn)

August, 1979: 35 + 125 v India, The Oval (Match drawn)

December, 1979: 0 + 99* v Australia, Perth (Australia won by 138 runs)

January, 1980: 8 + 18 v Australia, Sydney (Australia won by six wickets)

February, 1980: 44 + 7 v Australia, Melbourne (Australia won by eight wickets)

February, 1980: 22 + 43* v India, Mumbai (England won by 10 wickets)

June, 1980: 36 + 75 v West Indies, Trent Bridge (West Indies won by two wickets)

June, 1980: 8 + 49*; 0-11 v West Indies, Lord's (Match drawn)

July, 1980: 5 + 86 v West Indies, Old Trafford (Match drawn)

July, 1980: 53 + 5 v West Indies, The Oval (Match drawn)

August, 1980: 4 + 47 v West Indies, Headingley (Match drawn)

August, 1980: 62 + 128* v Australia, Lord's (Match drawn)

not out

118

February, 1981: 30 + 70 v West Indies, Port of Spain (West Indies won by an innings and 79 runs)

March, 1981: 0 + 1 v West Indies, Bridgetown (West Indies won by 298 runs)

March, 1981: 38 + 104* v West Indies, Antigua (Match drawn)

April, 1981: 40 + 12 v West Indies, Kingston (Match drawn)

June, 1981: 27 + 4 v Australia, Trent Bridge (Australia won by four wickets)

July, 1981: 17 + 60 v Australia, Lord's (Match drawn)

July, 1981: 12 + 46; 0-2 v Australia, Headingley (England won by 18 runs)

July, 1981: 13 + 29 v Australia, Edgbaston (England won by 29 runs)

August, 1981: 10 + 37 v Australia, Old Trafford (England won by 103 runs)

August, 1981: 137 + 0 v Australia, The Oval (Match drawn)

November, 1981: 60 + 3 v India, Mumbai (India won by 138 runs)

December, 1981: 36 + 50 v India, Bangalore (Match drawn)

December, 1981: 105 + 34* v India, Delhi (Match drawn)

January, 1982: 18 + 6 v India, Kolkata (Match drawn)

BRIAN CLOSE

July, 1949: 0; 1-39/0-46 v New Zealand, Old Trafford (Match drawn)

December, 1950: 0 + 1; 1-20/0-8 v Australia, Melbourne (Australia won by 28 runs)

August, 1955: 32 + 15 v South Africa, The Oval (England won by 92 runs)

May, 1957: 15 + 42; 0-8 v West Indies, Edgbaston (Match drawn)

June, 1957: 32 v West Indies, Lord's (England won by an innings and 36 runs)

July, 1959: 27; 1-18/4-35 v India, Headingley (England won by an innings and 173 runs)

July, 1961: 33 + 8; 0-33 v Australia, Old Trafford (Australia won by 54 runs)

June, 1963: 30 + 32; 0-31 v West Indies, Old Trafford (West Indies won by 10 wickets)

June, 1963: 9 + 70; 0-21 v West Indies, Lord's (Match drawn)

July, 1963: 5 + 55 v West Indies, Edgbaston (England won by 217 runs)

July, 1963: 0 +56 v West Indies, Headingley (West Indies won by 221 runs)

July, 1963: 46 + 4; 0-36 v West Indies, The Oval (West Indies won by eight wickets)

August, 1966: 4; 1-21/0-7 v West Indies, The Oval (England won by an innings and 34 runs)

June, 1967: 22*; 0-0/2-48 v India, Headingley (England won by six wickets)

June, 1967: 7; 2-28 v India, Lord's (England won by an innings and 124 runs)

July, 1967: 26+47; 4-68 v India, Edgbaston (England won by 132 runs)

July 1967: 4 + 36; 0-10/0-13 v Pakistan, Lord's (Match drawn)

August, 1967: 41; 0-12/1-11 v Pakistan, Trent Bridge (England won by 10 wickets)

August, 1967: 6 + 8; 0-15/1-4 v Pakistan, The Oval (England won by eight wickets)

June, 1976: 2 + 36* v West Indies, Trent Bridge (Match drawn)

June, 1976: 60 + 46 v West Indies, Lord's (Match drawn)

July, 1976: 2 + 20 v West Indies, Manchester (West Indies won by 425 runs)

RICHARD DAWSON

December, 2001: 5 + 11; 4-134 v India, Mohali (India won by 10 wickets)

December, 2001: 9 + 2; 0-73/2-72 v India, Ahmadabad (Match drawn)

December, 2001: 0* v India, Bangalore (Match drawn)

November, 2002: 6 + 19; 2-143 v Australia, Adelaide (Australia won by an innings and 51 runs)

November, 2002: 19* + 8; 0-21 v Australia, Perth (Australia won by an innings and 48 runs)

December, 2002: 6 + 15*; 2-121 v Australia, Melbourne (Australia won by five wickets)

January, 2003: 2 + 12; 0-72/1-41v Australia, Sydney (England won by 225 runs)

DARREN GOUGH

June, 1994: 65; 4-47/2-105 v New Zealand, Old Trafford (Match drawn)

July, 1994: 12 + 0*; 4-76/4-46 v South Africa, Lord's (South Africa won by 356 runs)

August, 1994: 27; 2-153/0-15 v South Africa, Headingley (Match drawn)

August, 1994: 42*; 0-85/1-39 v South Africa, The Oval (England won by eight wickets)

November, 1994: 17* + 10; 4-107/2-78 v Australia, Brisbane (Australia won by 184 runs)

December, 1994: 20 + 0; 4-60/3-59   v Australia, Melbourne (Australia won by 295 runs)

January, 1995: 51; 6-49/1-72 v Australia, Sydney (Match drawn)

June, 1995: 0 + 29; 1-24 v West Indies, Headingley (West Indies won by nine wickets)

June, 1995: 11 + 20; 2-84/3-79 v West Indies, Lord's (England won by 72 runs)

July, 1995: 1 + 12; 0-68 v West Indies, Edgbaston (West Indies won by an innings and 64 runs)

November, 1995: 0 v South Africa, Centurion (Match drawn)

November, 1995: 2; 0-64/0-48 v South Africa, Johannesburg (Match drawn)

December, 1996: 2 + 3*; 1-87/2-44 v Zimbabwe, Bulawayo (Match drawn)

December, 1996: 2; 4-40 v Zimbabwe, Harare (Match drawn)

January, 1997: 2; 4-91/2-66 v New Zealand, Auckland (Match drawn)

February, 1997: 18; 4-45/4-52 v New Zealand, Wellington (England won by an innings and 68 runs)

February, 1997: 0; 1-70/3-42 v New Zealand, Christchurch (England won by four wickets)

June, 1997: 0; 3-43/3-123 v Australia, Edgbaston (England won by nine wickets)

June, 1997: 10; 2-82 v Australia, Lord's (Match drawn)

July, 1997: 1 + 6; 3-52/0-62 v Australia, Old Trafford (Australia won by 268 runs)

July, 1997: 0 + 0; 5-149 v Australia, Headingley (Australia

italic * not out

119

won by an innings and 61 runs)

June, 1998: 16* (broken finger) v South Africa, Edgbaston (Match drawn)

July, 1998: 6 + 12; 3-116 v South Africa, Old Trafford (Match drawn)

July, 1998: 2; 4-116/1-56 v South Africa, Trent Bridge (England won by eight wickets)

August, 1998: 2 + 5; 3-58/6-42 v South Africa, Headingley (England won by 23 runs)

August, 1998: 4 + 15; 2-102 v Sri Lanka, The Oval (Sri Lanka won by 10 wickets)

November, 1998: 0; 1-135/0-50 v Australia, Brisbane (Match drawn)

December, 1998: 11 + 0; 3-43/1-18 v Australia, Perth (Australia won by seven wickets)

December, 1998: 7 + 3; 3-103/2-76v Australia, Adelaide (Australia won by 205 runs)

December, 1998: 11 + 4; 5-96/2-54v Australia, Melbourne (England won by 12 runs)

January, 1999: 0 + 7*; 3-61/1-51 v Australia, Sydney (Australia won by 98 runs)

November, 1999: 15* + 16*; 5-70 v South Africa, Johannesburg (South Africa won by an innings and 21 runs)

December, 1999: 6; 1-107/1-52 v South Africa, Port Elizabeth (Match drawn)

December, 1999: 9; 2-36/1-82 v South Africa, Durban (Match drawn)

January, 2000: 4 + 8; 2-88 v South Africa, Cape Town (South Africa won by an innings and 37 runs)

January, 2000: 6*; 2-92 v South Africa, Centurion (England won by two wickets)

May, 2000: 5; 2-36/4-57 v Zimbabwe, Lord's (England won by an innings and 209 runs)

June, 2000: 9 + 3; 3-66/0-15 v Zimbabwe, Trent Bridge (Match drawn)

June, 2000: 23 + 23*; 5-109 v West Indies, Edgbaston (West Indies won by an innings and 93 runs)

June, 2000: 13 + 4*; 4-72/2-17 v West Indies, Lord's (England won by two wickets)

August, 2000: 12; 2-58/1-96 v West Indies, Old Trafford (Match drawn)

August, 2000: 2; 3-59/4-30 v West Indies, Headingley (England won by an innings and 39 runs)

August, 2000: 8 + 1*; 1-25/3-64 v West Indies, The Oval (England won by 158 runs)

November, 2000: 0-45 v Pakistan, Lahore (Match drawn)

November, 2000: 19*; 3-79/1-32 v Pakistan, Faisalabad (Match drawn)

December, 2000: 18; 3-82/3-30 v Pakistan, Karachi (England won by six wickets)

February, 2001: 0* + 0; 1-95 v Sri Lanka, Galle (Sri Lanka won by an innings and 28 runs)

March, 2001: 10; 4-73/4-50 v Sri Lanka, Kandy (England won by three wickets)

March, 2001: 14; 2-33/3-23 v Sri Lanka, Colombo (SSC) (England won by four wickets)

May, 2001: 5*; 5-61/3-40 v Pakistan, Lord's (England won by an innings and nine runs)

May, 2001: 0 + 23; 3-94/3-85 v Pakistan, Old Trafford (Pakistan won by 108 runs)

July, 2001: 0 + 0; 3-152 v Australia, Edgbaston (Australia won by an innings 118 runs)

July 2001: 5 + 1; 3-115/1-5 v Australia, Lord's (Australia won by eight wickets)

August, 2001: 0 * + 5*; 2-63/0-38 v Australia, Trent Bridge (Australia won by seven wickets)

August, 2001: 8; 5-103/2-68 v Australia, Headingley (England won by six wickets)

August, 2001: 24 + 39*; 1-113 v Australia, The Oval (Australia won by an innings and 25 runs)

July 2003: 1; 1-88 v South Africa, Edgbaston (Match drawn)

July, 2003: 34 + 14; 0-127 v South Africa, Lord's (South Africa won by an innings and 92 runs)

JOHN HAMPSHIRE

June, 1969: 107 + 5 v West Indies, Lord's (Match drawn)

July, 1969: 1 + 22 v West Indies, Headingley (England won by 30 runs)

January, 1971: 55 + 3 v Australia, Adelaide (Match drawn)

February, 1971: 10 + 24 v Australia, Sydney (England won by 62 runs)

February, 1971: 40 + 51* v New Zealand, Christchurch (England won by eight wickets)

March, 1971: 9 + 0 v New Zealand, Auckland (Match drawn)

August, 1972: 42 + 20 v Australia, The Oval (Australia won by five wickets)

August, 1975: 14 + 0 v Australia, Headingley (Match drawn after abandonment)

MATTHEW HOGGARD

June, 2000: 12*; 0-49 v West Indies, Lord's (England won by two wickets)

May, 2001: 0 + 0*; 3-79/3-93 v Pakistan, Old Trafford (England lost by 108 runs)

December, 2001: 0 + 0*; 3-98/0-5 v Pakistan, Mohali (India won by ten wickets)

December, 2001:4* + 1; 2-65/0-33 v India, Ahmedabad (Match drawn)

December, 2001: 1; 4-80 v India, Bangalore (Match drawn)

March, 2002: 0*; 7-63/1-142 v New Zealand, Christchurch (England won by 98 runs)

March, 2002: 7; 0-32/2-31 v New Zealand, Wellington (Match drawn)

March, 2002: 0 + 2; 3-66/4-68 v New Zealand, Auckland (England lost by 78 runs)

May, 2002: 0*; 2-160 v Sri Lanka, Lord's (Match drawn)

May, 2002: 17*; 2-55/5-92 v Sri Lanka, Edgbaston (England won by an innings and 111 runs)

June, 2002: 7; 3-38/2-97 v Sri Lanka, Old Trafford (England won by ten wickets)

July, 2002: 10*; 3-33/4-87 v India, Lord's (England won by 170 runs)

August, 2002: 32; 4-105/1-09 v India, Trent Bridge (Match drawn)

August, 2002: 0 + 1*; 1-102 v India, Headingley (India won by an innings and 46 runs)

September, 2002: 0; 1-97 v India, The Oval (Match drawn)

November, 2002: 4 + 1*; 0-122/0-42 v Australia, Brisbane (Australia won by 384 runs)

not out

November, 2002: 6 + 1; 1-84 v Australia, Adelaide (Australia won by an innings and 51 runs)

January, 2003: 0 + 0; 4-92/1-35 v Australia, Sydney (England won by 225 runs)

May, 2003: 19; 3-24/0-35 v Zimbabwe, Lord's (England won by an innings and 92 runs)

October, 2003: 6*; 3-55/4-48 v Bangladesh, Dhaka, (England won by seven wickets)

October, 2003: 0*; 1-64/1-37 v Bangladesh, Chittagong (England won by 329 runs)

December, 2003: 6* + 0*; 0-49/1-33 v Sri Lanka, Galle (Match drawn)

March, 2004: 9*; 3-68/2-21 v West Indies, Kingston (England won by ten wickets)

March, 2004: 0*; 1-38/2-48 v West Indies, Port of Spain (England won by seven wickets)

April, 2004: 0; 1-34/4-35 v West Indies, Bridgetown (England won by eight wickets)

April, 2004: 1; 0-82 v West Indies, St John's (Match drawn)

May, 2004: 15; 1-68/0-39 v New Zealand, Lord's (England won by seven wickets)

June, 2004: 4; 2-93/4-75 v New Zealand, Headingley (England won by nine wickets)

June, 2004: 5; 2-85/0-25 v New Zealand, Trent Bridge (England won by four wickets)

July, 2004: 1*; 2-89/2-65 v West Indies, Lord's (England won by 210 runs)

July, 2004: 15* + 6; 3-89/3-64 v West Indies, Edgbaston (England won by 256 runs)

August, 2004: 23; 4-83/0-21 v West Indies, Old Trafford (England won by seven wickets)

August, 2004: 38; 1-31/1-50 v West Indies, The Oval (England won by ten wickets)

December, 2004: 0; 3-56/1-38 v South Africa, Port Elizabeth (England won by seven wickets)

December, 2004: 6*; 3-58/2-58 v South Africa, Durban (Match drawn)

January, 2005: 1 + 7*; 2-87/1-46 v South Africa, Cape Town (South Africa won by 196 runs)

January, 2005: 5 + 0; 5-144/7-61

v South Africa, Johannesburg (England won by 77 runs)

January, 2005: 1; 1-64/1-51 v South Africa, Centurion (Match drawn)

May, 2005: 4-42/2-42 v Bangladesh, Lord's (England won by an innings and 261 runs)

June, 2005: 3-24/5-73 v Bangladesh, Riverside (England won by an innings and 27 runs)

July, 2005: 0 + 0; 1-40/2-56 v Australia, Lord's (Australia won by 239 runs)

August, 2005: 16 + 1; 1-41/1-26 v Australia, Edgbaston (England won by two runs)

August, 2005: 4; 0-22/ 2-49 v Australia, Old Trafford (Match drawn)

August, 2005: 10 + 8*; 3-70/2-72 v Australia, Trent Bridge (England won by three wickets)

September, 2005: 2 + 4*; 4-97 v Australia, The Oval (Match drawn)

November, 2005: 1 + 0*; 2-55/2-81 v Pakistan, Multan (Pakistan won by 22 runs)

November, 2005: 2; 2-115/3-50 v Pakistan, Faisalabad (Match drawn)

November, 2005: 1* + 0; 2-106 v Pakistan, Lahore (Pakistan won by innings and 100 runs)

March, 2006: 11; 6-57/1-29 v India, Nagpur (Match drawn)

March, 2006: 4* + 4; 2-55/1-24 v India, Mohali (India won by nine wickets)

March, 2006: 0 + 6; 2-54/1-13 v India, Mumbai (England won by 212 runs)

May, 2006: 7; 4-27/2-110 v Sri Lanka, Lord's (Match drawn)

May, 2006: 3; 2-32/3-64 v Sri Lanka, Edgbaston (England won by six wickets)

June, 2006: 10 + 4; 2-65/2-71 v Sri Lanka, Trent Bridge (Sri Lanka won by 134 runs)

July, 2006: 2 + 12*; 3-117/2-31 v Pakistan, Lord's (Match drawn)

August, 2006: 6; 0-30/0-52 v Pakistan, Old Trafford (England won by an innings and 120 runs)

August, 2006: 0 + 8; 1-93/1-26 v Pakistan, Headingley (England won by 167 runs)

August, 2006: 3; 3-124 v Pakistan, The Oval (England awarded

match)

November, 2006: 0 + 8; 2-98/0-43 v Australia, Brisbane (Australia won by 277 runs)

December, 2006: 4; 7-109/1-29 v Australia, Adelaide (Australia won by six wickets)

December, 2006: 4 + 0; 1-40/1-85 v Australia, Perth (Australia won by 206 runs)

December, 2006: 9* + 5; 1-82 v Australia, Melbourne (Australia won by an innings and 99 runs)

May, 2007: 0-29 v West Indies, Lord's (Match drawn)

June, 2007: 0; 2-58/3-28 v West Indies, Riverside (England won by seven wickets)

December, 2007: 15 + 8; 4-29/2-55   v Sri Lanka, Kandy (Sri Lanka won by 88 runs)

December, 2007: 0; 1-121 v Sri Lanka, Galle (Match drawn)

March, 2008: 2 + 4; 1-122/0-29 v New Zealand, Hamilton (New Zealand won by 189 runs)

RAY ILLINGWORTH

July 1958: 3*; 1-39/2-20 v New Zealand, Old Trafford (England won by an innings and 13 runs)

July, 1959: 21 + 47*; 2-16/1-63 v India, Old Trafford (England won by 171 runs)

August, 1959: 50; 0-2/1-43 v India, The Oval (England won by an innings and 27 runs)

January, 1960: 5; 0-106 v West Indies, Bridgetown (Match drawn)

January, 1960: 10 + 41*; 0-8/0-38 v West Indies, Port of Spain (England won by 256 runs)

February, 1960: 17 + 6; 2-46/0-35 v West Indies, Kingston (Match drawn)

March, 1960: 4 + 9; 0-72 v West Indies, Georgetown (Match drawn)

March, 1960: 0; 0-25/2-53 v West Indies, Port of Spain (Match drawn)

June, 1960: 1 + 16; 3-15/3-57 v South Africa, Edgbaston (England won by 100 runs)

June, 1960: 0*; 0-0 v South Africa, Lord's (England won by an innings and 73 runs)

July, 1960: 37; 0-33 v South Africa, Trent Bridge (England won by eight wickets)

not out

121

July, 1960: 22* + 5; 0-35/0-6 v South Africa, Old Trafford (Match drawn)

June, 1961: 15; 2-110 v Australia, Edgbaston (Match drawn)

June, 1961: 13 + 0; 1-16 v Australia, Lord's (Australia won by five wickets)

August, 1962: 2*; 0-27/1-54 v Pakistan, The Oval (England won by ten wickets)

January, 1963: 12; 1-85/0-23 v Australia, Adelaide (Match drawn)

February, 1963: 27 + 18; 0-15/0-8 v Australia, Sydney (Match drawn)

February, 1963: 20; 0-5/4-34 v New Zealand, Auckland (England won by an innings and 215 runs)

March, 1963: 46; 1-34 v New Zealand, Wellington (England won by an innings and 47 runs)

March, 1963: 2 v New Zealand, Christchurch (England won by seven wickets)

June, 1965: 4-42/0-28 v New Zealand, Headingley (England won by an innings and 187)

June, 1966: 0 + 4; 0-21/0-82 v West Indies, Trent Bridge (West Indies won by 139 runs)

August, 1966: 3; 2-40/2-22 v West Indies, The Oval (England won by an innings and 34 runs)

June, 1967: 12*; 3-31/4-100 v India, Headingley (England won by six wickets)

June, 1967: 4; 1-0/6-29 v India, Lord's (England won by an innings and 124 runs)

July, 1967: 2 + 10; 2-14/4-92 v India, Edgbaston (England won by 132 runs)

July, 1967: 4 + 9; 2-48/1-10 v Pakistan, Lord's (Match drawn)

July, 1968: 27; 3-37/0-4 v Australia, Edgbaston (Match drawn)

July, 1968: 6; 1-47/6-87 v Australia, Headingley (Match Drawn)

August, 1968: 8 + 10; 2-87/1-29 v Australia, The Oval (England won by 226 runs)

June, 1969: 21; 0-23/1-52 v West Indies, Old Trafford (England won by 10 wickets)

June, 1969: 113 + 9*; 0-39/3-66 v West Indies, Lord's (Match drawn)

July, 1969: 1 + 19; 1-38 v West Indies, Headingley (England won

by 30 runs)

July, 1969: 53 + 0; 4-37/0-24 v New Zealand, Lord's (England won by 230 runs)

August, 1969: 33; 2-15/1-3 v New Zealand, Trent Bridge (Match drawn)

August, 1969: 4; 3-55/0-20 v New Zealand, The Oval (England won by eight wickets)

November, 1970: 8; 0-47/1-19 v Australia, Brisbane (Match drawn)

December, 1970: 34 + 29; 1-43/0-12 v Australia, Perth (Match drawn)

January, 1971: 25 + 53; 1-59/0-9 v Australia, Sydney (England won by 299 runs)

January, 1971: 41; 2-59 v Australia, Melbourne (Match drawn)

January, 1971: 24 + 48*; 1-14/0-32 v Australia, Adelaide (Match drawn)

February, 1971: 42 + 29; 1-16/3-39 v Australia, Sydney (England won by 62 runs)

February, 1971: 36; 0-12/0-45 v New Zealand, Christchurch (England won by eight wickets)

February, 1971: 0 + 22; 0-45 v New Zealand, Auckland (Match drawn)

June, 1971: 1 + 1; 3-72 v Pakistan, Edgbaston (Match drawn)

June, 1971: 0-1 v Pakistan, Lord's (Match drawn)

July, 1971: 20 + 45; 0-31/3-58 v Pakistan, Headingley (England won by 25 runs)

July, 1971: 33+ 20; 0-43/2-33 v India, Lord's (Match drawn)

August, 1971: 107; 0-16 v India, Old Trafford (Match drawn)

August, 1971: 11 + 4; 5-70/0-40 v India, The Oval: (India won by four wickets)

June, 1972: 26* + 14 v Australia, Old Trafford (England won by 89 runs)

June, 1972: 30 + 12; 1-13 v Australia, Lord's (Australia won by eight wickets)

July, 1972: 24*; 1-41 v Australia, Trent Bridge (Match drawn)

July, 1972: 57; 2-32/2-32 v Australia, Headingley (England won by nine wickets)

August, 1972: 0 + 31; 1-53/0-26 v

Australia, The Oval (Australia won by five wickets)

June, 1973: 8 + 3; 0-31 v New Zealand, Trent Bridge (England won by 38 runs)

June, 1973: 3 + 22; 0-87 v New Zealand, Lord's (Match drawn)

July, 1973: 65; 0-20/0-1 v New Zealand, Headingley (England won by an innings and one run)

July, 1973: 27 + 40; 0-43/3-50 v West Indies, The Oval (West Indies won by 158 runs)

August, 1973: 27; 1-37/1-67 v West Indies, Edgbaston (Match drawn)

August, 1973: 0-13/1-114 v West Indies, Lord's (West Indies won by an innings and 226 runs)

PAUL JARVIS

February, 1988: 14 + 10*; 2-43/1-30 v New Zealand, Christchurch (Match drawn)

February, 1988: 10; 2-74/1-54 v New Zealand, Auckland (Match drawn)

June, 1988: 6; 2-63 v West Indies, Trent Bridge (Match drawn)

June, 1988: 7 + 29*; 3-26/4-107 v West Indies, Lord's (West Indies won by 134 runs)

June, 1989: 6 + 5; 1-150/0-38 v Australia, Lord's (Australia won by six wickets)

July, 1989: 22; 0-82/1-20 v Australia, Edgbaston (Match drawn)

January, 1993: 4 + 6; 2-72/0-23 v India, Kolkata (India won by eight wickets)

February, 1993: 8 + 2; 2-72 v India, Chennai (India won by an innings and 22 runs)

March, 1993: 0 + 3; 3-76/0-14 v Sri Lanka, Colombo (Sri Lanka won by five wickets)

MARTYN MOXON

July, 1986: 74 + 5 v New Zealand, Lord's (Match drawn)

August, 1986: 9 + 23 v New Zealand, Trent Bridge (New Zealand won by eight wickets)

August, 1987: 8 + 15; 0-27 v Pakistan, The Oval (Match drawn)

January, 1988: 40 v Australia, Sydney (Match drawn)

February, 1988: 1 + 27 v New

italic *not out*

Zealand, Christchurch (Match drawn)

February, 1988: 99; 0-3 v New Zealand, Auckland (Match drawn)

March, 1988: 81* v New Zealand, Wellington (Match drawn)

June, 1988: 26 + 14 v West Indies, Lord's (West Indies won by 134 runs)

June, 1988: 0 + 15 v West Indies, Old Trafford (West Indies won by an innings and 156 runs)

August, 1989: 2 + 6 v Australia, Trent Bridge (Australia won by an innings and 180 runs)

CHRIS OLD

December, 1972: 33* + 17*; 2-72/4-43 v India, Kolkata (India won by 28 runs)

January, 1972: 4 + 9; 0-51/2-19 v India, Chennai (India won by four wickets)

January, 1973: 4; 4-69/0-28 v India, Kanpur (Match drawn)

February, 1973: 28; 3-78/0-11 v India, Mumbai (Match drawn)

March, 1973: 0 + 17*; 0-98 v Pakistan, Lahore (Match drawn)

June, 1973: 7 + 7; 5-113 v New Zealand, Lord's (Match drawn)

July, 1973: 34; 4-71/2-41 v New Zealand, Headingley (England won by an innings and one run).

August, 1973: 0; 3-86/1-65 v West Indies, Edgbaston (Match drawn)

February, 1974: 11 + 3; 3-89/0-18 v West Indies, Trinidad (West Indies won by seven wickets)

February, 1974: 2 + 19; 2-72 v West Indies, Jamaica (Match drawn)

March, 1974: 1 + 0; 0-102 v West Indies, Barbados (Match drawn)

March, 1974: 14; 0-32 v West Indies, Guyana (Match drawn)

June, 1974: 12; 1-46/4-20 v India, Old Trafford (England won by 113 runs)

June, 1974: 3; 4-67/5-21 v India, Lord's (England won by an innings and 285 runs)

July, 1974: 1-43/3-52 v India, Edgbaston (England won by an innings at 78 runs)

July, 1974: 0 + 10*; 3-65/3-54 v Pakistan, Headingley (Match drawn)

August, 1974: 41; 0-17/0-39 v

Pakistan, Lord's (Match drawn)

August, 1974: 65; 0-143/1-6 v Pakistan, The Oval (Match drawn)

December, 1974: 7 + 43; 3-85 v Australia, Perth (Australia won by nine wickets)

December, 1974: 0; 3-50/0-75 v Australia, Melbourne (England won by an innings and four runs)

February, 1975: 9*; 1-17 v New Zealand, Auckland (England won by an innings and 83 runs)

July, 1975: 13 + 7; 2-111 v Australia, Edgbaston (Australia won by an innings and 85 runs)

August, 1975: 5 + 10; 1-30/1-61 v Australia, Headingley (Match drawn)

August, 1975: 25* + 0; 3-74/0-7 v Australia, The Oval (Match drawn)

June, 1976: 33; 3-80/1-64 v West Indies, Trent Bridge (Match drawn)

June, 1976: 19 + 13; 1-58/1-46 v West Indies, Lord's (Match drawn)

December, 1976: 15; 2-28/0-6 v India, Delhi (England won by an innings and 25 runs)

January, 1977: 52; 2-37/3-38 v India, Kolkata (England won by 10 wickets)

January, 1977: 2 + 4; 2-19/0-11 v India, Chennai (England won by 200 runs)

January, 1977: 9 + 13; 0-43/1-19 v India, Bangalore (India won by 140 runs)

March, 1977: 3 + 2; 3-39/4-104 v Australia, Melbourne, Centenary Test (Australia won by 45 runs)

June, 1977: 9 + 0; 2-70/2-46 v Australia, Lord's (Match drawn)

July, 1977: 37; 1-57/0-26 v Australia, Old Trafford (England won by nine wickets)

December, 1977: 2; 1-63/0-18 v Pakistan, Lahore (Match drawn)

February, 1978: 10 + 9; 6-54/1-32 v New Zealand, Wellington (New Zealand won by 72 runs)

February, 1978: 8 + 1; 0-55/1-9 v New Zealand, Christchurch (England won by 174 runs)

June, 1978: 5; 7-50/1-38 v Pakistan, Edgbaston (England won by an innings and 57 runs)

June, 1978: 0; 1-26/0-36 v Pakistan, Lord's (England won by an innings and 120 runs)

June, 1978: 4-41 v Pakistan, Headingley (Match drawn)

July, 1978: 16; 1-43/0-13 v New Zealand, The Oval (England won by seven wickets)

December, 1978: 29*; 2-24/2-60 v Australia, Brisbane (England won by seven wickets)

August, 1980: 6; 2-64 v West Indies, Headingley (Match drawn)

August, 1980: 24*; 3-91/3-47 v Australia, Lord's Centenary Test (Match drawn)

February, 1981: 1 + 0; 1-49 v West Indies, Trinidad (West Indies won by an innings and 79 runs)

July, 1981: 0 + 29; 0-91/1-21 v Australia, Headingley (England won by 18 runs)

July, 1981: 11* + 23; 3-44/1-19 v Australia, Edgbaston (England won by 29 runs)

PHIL SHARPE

July, 1963: 23 + 85* v West Indies, Edgbaston (England won by 217 runs)

July, 1963: 0 + 13 v West Indies, Headingley (West Indies won by 221 runs)

August, 1963: 63 + 83 v West Indies, The Oval (West Indies won by eight wickets)

January, 1964: 27 + 31* v India, Chennai (Match drawn)

June, 1964: 35* + 1 v Australia, Trent Bridge (Match drawn)

June, 1964: 35 v Australia, Lord's (Match drawn)

June, 1969: 2 v West Indies, Old Trafford (England won by 10 wickets)

June, 1969: 11 + 86 v West Indies, Lord's (Match drawn)

July, 1969: 6 + 15 v West Indies, Headingley (England won by 30 runs)

July, 1969: 20 + 46 v New Zealand, Lord's (England won by 230 runs)

August, 1969: 111 v New Zealand, Trent Bridge (Match drawn)

August, 1969: 48 + 45* v New Zealand, The Oval (England won by eight wickets)

ARNIE SIDEBOTTOM

July, 1985: 2; 1-65 v Australia at Trent Bridge (Match drawn)

italic * not out

123

CHRIS SILVERWOOD

December, 1996: 0; 3-63/1-8 v Zimbabwe, Bulawayo (Match drawn)

December, 1999: 6; 1-57/0-24 v South Africa, Port Elizabeth (Match drawn)

December, 1999: 0; 0-38/0-89 v South Africa, Durban (Match drawn)

January, 2000: 1 + 5*; 5-91 v South Africa, Cape Town (South Africa won by an innings and 37 runs)

January, 2000: 1-45 v South Africa, Centurion (England won by two wickets)

November, 2002: 10; 0-29 v Australia, Perth (Australia won an innings and 48 runs)

KEN TAYLOR

June, 1959: 24 v India at Trent Bridge (England won by an innings at 59 runs)

June, 1959: 6 + 3 v India at Lord's (England won by eight wickets)

July, 1964: 9 + 15; 0-16 v Australia at Headingley (Australia won by seven wickets)

MICHAEL VAUGHAN

November, 1999: 35 + 5; 0-39 v South Africa, Johannesburg (South Africa won by an innings and 21 runs)

December, 1999: 21 + 29; 0-16/0-9 v South Africa, Port Elizabeth (Match drawn)

January, 2000: 42 + 5 v South Africa, Cape Town (South Africa won by an innings and 37 runs)

January, 2000: 69; 0-9 v South Africa, Centurion (England won by two wickets)

June, 2000: 4 + 41; 0-10 v West Indies, Lord's (England won by two wickets)

August, 2000: 29; 0-3 v West Indies, Old Trafford (Match drawn)

August, 2000: 76 v West Indies, Headingley (England won by an innings and 39 runs)

August, 2000: 10 + 9; 0-12 v West Indies, The Oval (England won by 158 runs)

March, 2001: 26 + 8 v Sri Lanka, Colombo (SSC) (England won by four wickets)

May, 2001: 32; 0-12 v Pakistan, Lord's (England won by an innings and nine runs)

May, 2001: 120 + 14; 0-21 v Pakistan, Old Trafford (England lost by 108 runs)

December, 2001: 11 + 31* v India, Ahmedabad (Match drawn)

December, 2001: 64 v India, Bangalore (Match drawn)

March, 2002: 27 + 0 v New Zealand, Christchurch (England won by 98 runs)

March, 2002: 7 + 34; 0-15 v New Zealand, Wellington (Match drawn)

March, 2002: 27 + 36 v New Zealand, Auckland (England lost by 78 runs)

May, 2002: 64 + 115; 0-35 v Sri Lanka, Lord's (Match drawn)

May, 2002: 46 v Sri Lanka, Edgbaston (England won by an innings and 111 runs)

June, 2002: 36; 0-9 v Sri Lanka, Old Trafford (England won by ten wickets)

July, 2002: 0 + 100; 1-12 v India, Lord's (England won by 170 runs)

August, 2002: 197; 2-71 v India, Trent Bridge (Match drawn)

August, 2002: 61 + 15; 0-1 v India, Headingley (India won by an innings and 146 runs)

September, 2002: 195 + 47*; 1-36 v India, The Oval (Match drawn)

November, 2002: 33 + 0 v Australia, Brisbane (Australia won by 384 runs) November, 2002: 177 + 41 v Australia, Adelaide (Australia won by an innings and 51 runs)

November, 2002: 34 + 9 v Australia, Perth (Australia won by an innings and 48 runs)

December, 2002: 11 + 145 v Australia, Melbourne (Australia won by five wickets)

January, 2003: 0 + 183 v Australia, Sydney (England won by 225 runs)

May, 2003: 8 v Zimbabwe, Lord's (England won by an innings and 92 runs)

June, 2003: 20 v Zimbabwe, Riverside (England won by an innings and 69 runs)

July, 2003: 156 + 22; 1-26 v South Africa, Edgbaston (Match drawn)

July, 2003: 33 + 29 v South Africa, Lord's (South Africa won by an innings and 92 runs)

August, 2003: 1 + 5; 0-0 v South Africa, Trent Bridge (England won by 70 runs)

August, 2003: 15 + 21; 0-13 v South Africa, Headingley (South Africa won by 191 runs)

September, 2003: 23 + 13; 0-24 v South Africa, The Oval (England won by nine wickets)

October, 2003: 48 + 81* v Bangladesh, Dhaka, (England won by seven wickets)

October, 2003: 54 + 25 v Bangladesh, Chittagong (England won by 329 runs)

December, 2003: 24 + 8; 0-2 v Sri Lanka, Galle (Match drawn)

December, 2003: 52 + 105; 0-9/0-11 v Sri Lanka, Kandy (Match drawn)

December, 2003: 18 + 14; 0-5 v Sri Lanka, Colombo (SCC) (Sri Lanka won by an innings and 215 runs)

March, 2004: 15 + 11*; 0-2 v West Indies, Kingston (England won by ten wickets)

March, 2004: 0 + 23 v West Indies, Port of Spain (England won by seven wickets)

April, 2004: 17 + 32 v West Indies, Bridgetown (England won by eight wickets)

April, 2004: 7 + 140; 0-60 v West Indies, St John's (Match drawn)

June, 2004: 13; 0-3 v New Zealand, Headingley (England won by nine wickets)

June, 2004: 61 + 10; 0-5 v New Zealand, Trent Bridge (England won by four wickets)

July, 2004: 103 + 101* v West Indies, Lord's (England won by 210 runs)

July, 2004: 12 + 3; 0-8/0-9 v West Indies, Edgbaston (England won by 256 runs)

August, 2004: 12 + 33 v West Indies, Old Trafford (England won by seven wickets)

August, 2004: 66 v West Indies, The Oval (England won by ten wickets)

December, 2004: 10 + 15 v South Africa, Port Elizabeth (England won by seven wickets)

December, 2004: 18 + 10; 1-29/0-0 v South Africa, Durban (Match

not out

drawn)

January, 2005: 11 + 20 v South Africa, Cape Town (South Africa won by 196 runs)

January, 2005: 82* + 54 v South Africa, Johannesburg (England won by 77 runs)

January, 2005: 0 + 26* v South Africa, Centurion (Match drawn)

May, 2005: 120 v Bangladesh, Lord's (England won by an innings and 261 runs)

June, 2005: 44 v Bangladesh, Riverside (England won by an innings and 27 runs)

July, 2005: 3 + 4 v Australia, Lord's (Australia won by 239 runs)

August, 2005: 24 + 1 v Australia, Edgbaston (England won by two runs)

August, 2005: 166 + 14; 0-21 v Australia, Old Trafford (Match drawn)

August, 2005: 58 + 0 v Australia, Trent Bridge (England won by three wickets)

September, 2005: 11 + 45 v Australia, The Oval (Match drawn)

November, 2005: 2 + 9 v Pakistan, Faisalabad (Match drawn)

November, 2005: 58 + 13 v Pakistan, Lahore (Pakistan won by innings and 100 runs)

May, 2007: 103 v West Indies, Headingley (England won by an innings and 283 runs)

June, 2007: 41 + 40 v West Indies, Old Trafford (England won by 60 runs)

June, 2007: 19 + 48* v West Indies, Riverside (England won by seven wickets)

July, 2007: 79 + 30; 0-18 v India, Lord's (Match drawn)

July, 2007: 9 + 124 v India, Trent Bridge (India won by seven wickets)

August, 2007: 11 + 42 v India, The Oval (Match drawn)

December, 2007: 37 + 5; 0-6 v Sri Lanka, Kandy (Sri Lanka won by 88 runs)

December, 2007: 87 + 61 v Sri Lanka, Colombo (SSC) (Match drawn)

December, 2007: 1 + 24 v Sri Lanka, Galle (Match drawn)

March, 2008: 63 + 9 v New Zealand, Hamilton (New Zealand won by 189 runs)

March, 2008: 32 + 13 v New Zealand, Wellington (England won by 126 runs)

March, 2008: 2 + 4 v New Zealand, Napier (England won by 121 runs)

May, 2008: 106 v New Zealand, Lord's (Match drawn)

May, 2008: 30 + 48 v New Zealand, Old Trafford (England won by six wickets)

June, 2008: 16 v New Zealand, Trent Bridge (England won by an innings and nine runs)

July, 2008: 2 v South Africa, Lord's (Match drawn)

July, 2008: 0 + 21 v South Africa, Headingley (South Africa won by ten wickets)

July, 2008: 0 + 17 v South Africa, Edgbaston (South Africa won by five wickets)

CRAIG WHITE

June, 1994: 19; 1-38/0-0 v New Zealand, Trent Bridge (England won by an innings and 90 runs)

June, 1994: 51 + 9; 1-84/0-21 v New Zealand, Lord's (Match drawn)

June, 1994: 42; 3-18/1-36 v New Zealand, Old Trafford (Match drawn)

July, 1994: 10 + 0; 2-43/0-18 v South Africa, Lord's (South Africa won by 356 runs)

July, 1995: 23 + 1; 0-23/0-23 v West Indies, Old Trafford (England won by six wickets)

August, 1995: 1 + 1; 0-30 v West Indies, Trent Bridge (Match drawn)

December, 1996: 9; 1-41 v Zimbabwe, Harare (SC) (Match drawn)

January, 1997: 0; 2-51/0-26 v New Zealand, Auckland (Match drawn)

June, 2000: 27 + 0; 0-30 v West Indies, Lord's (England won by two wickets)

August, 2000: 6; 1-18/2-67 v West Indies, Old Trafford (Match drawn)

August, 2000: 0; 5-57 v West Indies, Headingley (England won by an innings and 39 runs)

August, 2000: 11* + 18; 5-32/0-32 v West Indies, The Oval (England won by 158 runs)

November, 2000: 93; 4-54 v Pakistan, Lahore (Match drawn)

November, 2000: 41 + 9*; 2-71/0-55 v Pakistan, Faisalabad (Match drawn)

December, 2000: 35; 1-64/2-30 v Pakistan, Karachi (England won by six wickets)

February, 2001: 25 + 3; 0-80 v Sri Lanka, Galle (Sri Lanka won by an innings and 28 runs)

March, 2001: 39 + 21*; 2-70/2-42 v Sri Lanka, Kandy (England won by three wickets)

March, 2001: 0 + 8; 0-45 v Sri Lanka, Colombo (SSC) (England won by four wickets)

July, 2001: 4 + 0; 1-101 v Australia, Edgbaston (Australia won by an innings and 118 runs)

July, 2001: 0 + 27*; 0-80 v Australia, Lord's (Australia won by eight wickets)

August, 2001: 0 + 7; 0-8 v Australia, Trent Bridge (Australia won by seven wickets)

December, 2001: 5 + 22; 1-56 v India, Mohali (India won by 10 wickets)

December, 2001: 121 + 18; 1-33/0-7 v India, Ahmedabad (Match drawn)

December, 2001: 39; 0-26 v India, Bangalore (Match drawn)

July, 2002: 53 + 6*; 2-46/2-61 v India, Lord's (England won by 170 runs)

August, 2002: 94*; 1-56/0-15 v India, Trent Bridge (Match drawn)

November, 2002: 12 + 13; 2-105/0-61 v Australia, Brisbane (Australia won by 384 runs)

November, 2002: 1 + 5; 4-106 v Australia, Adelaide (Australia won by an innings and 51 runs)

November, 2002: 2 + 15; 5-127 v Australia, Perth (Australia won by an innings and 48 runs)

December, 2002: 85* + 21; 3-133 v Australia, Melbourne (Australia won by five wickets)

not out

125

THE MATCHES: **ENGLAND V AUSTRALIA AT HEADINGLEY**

June, 1899:

Australia won toss and batted:

Australia: 172 (J Worrall 76; H Trumble 56) and 224; England 220 (AFA Lilley 55; H Trumble 5-60) and 19-0.

MATCH DRAWN

July, 1905:

England won toss and batted:

England 301 (F S Jackson 144 not out;) and 295 for five declared (JT Tyedsesley 100, TW Hayward 60; WW Armstrong 5-122). Australia 195 (WW Armstrong 66; Warren 5-57) and 224-7 (MA Noble 62)

MATCH DRAWN

July, 1909:

Australia won the toss and decided to bat

Australia 188 and 207 (SF Barnes 6-63); England 182 (JT Tyldesley 55, J Sharp 61; CG Macartney 7-58) and 87 (A Cotter 5-38)

AUSTRALIA WON BY 126 RUNS

July, 1921:

Australia won the toss and decided to bat.

Australia 407 (CG Macartney 115, W Armstrong 77, JM Taylor 50) and 273 (TJE Andrews 92). England 259 (JWHT Douglas 75, G Brown 57, Hon LH Tennyson 63) and 202.

AUSTRALIA WON BY 219 RUNS

July, 1926:

England won the toss and decided to field

Australia 494 (WM Woodfull, 141, CG Macartney 151, AJ Richardson 100). England 294 (GG Macauley 76; CV Grimmett 5-88) and (following on) 254-4 (JB Hobbs 88, H Sutcliffe 94)

MATCH DRAWN

July, 1930:

Australia won the toss and decided to bat

Australia 566 (W Woodfull 50, DG Bradman 334, AF Kippax 77; MW Tate 5-124). England 391 (WR Hammond 113; CV Grimmett 5-135) and (following on) 95-3

MATCH DRAWN

July, 1934:

England won the toss and decided to bat

England 200 and 229-6. Australia 584 (DG Bradman 304, WH Ponsford 181; WE Bowes 6-142)

MATCH DRAWN

July, 1938:

England won the toss and decided to bat

England 223 (WR Hammond 76; WJ O'Reilly 5-66) and 123 (WJ O'Reilly 5-56). Australia 242 (DG Bradman 103, BA Barnett 57) and 107-5.

AUSTRALIA WON BY FIVE WICKETS

July, 1948:

England won toss and decided to bat

England 496 (L Hutton 81, C Washbrook 143, WJ Edrich 111, AV Bedser 79) and 365-8 declared (L Hutton 57, C Washbrook 65, WJ Edrich 54, DCS Compton 66). Australia 458 (KR Miller 58, RN Harvey 112, SJE Loxton 93, RR Lindwall 77) and 404-3 (AR Morris 182, DG Bradman 173).

AUSTRALIA WON BY SEVEN WICKETS

July, 1953:

Australia won the toss and decided to field

England 167 (TW Graveney 55; RR Lindwall 5-54) and 275 (WJ Edrich 64, W Watson 61). Australia 266 (RN Harvey 71, GB Hole 53; AV Bedser 6-95) and 147-4

MATCH DRAWN

July, 1956:

England won the toss and decided to bat

England 325 (PBH May 101, C Washbrook 98. Australia 143 (JC Laker 5-58) and (following on) 140 (RN Harvey 69; JC Laker 6-55).

ENGLAND WON BY AN INNINGS AND 42 RUNS

July, 1961:

Australia won the toss and decided to bat

Australia 237 (CC McDonald 54, RN Harvey 73; FS Trueman 5-58) and 120 (RN Harvey 53; FS Trueman 6-30). England 299 (G Pullar 53, MC Cowdrey 93; AK Davidson 5-63) and 62-2

ENGLAND WON BY EIGHT WICKETS

July, 1964:

England won the toss and decided to bat

England 268 (ER Dexter 66; JM Parks 68; NJN Hawke 5-75) and 229 (KF Barrington 85). Australia 389 (WM Lawry 78, PJ Burge 160 and 111-3 (IR Redpath 58 not out)

AUSTRALIA WON BY SEVEN WICKETS

not out

July, 1968:

Australia won the toss and decided to bat:

Australia 315 (IR Redpath 92, IM Chappell 65) and 312 (KD Walters 56, IM Chappell 81; R Illingworth 6-87). England 302 (JH Edrich 62, RM Prideaux 64; AN Connolly 5-72) and 230-4 (JH Edrich 65)

MATCH DRAWN

July, 1972:

Australia won the toss and decided to bat:

Australia 146 (KR Stackpole 52) and 136 (DL Underwood 6-45). England 263 (R Illingworth 57; AA Mallett 5-114) and 21-.

ENGLAND WON BY NINE WICKETS

August, 1975:

England won the toss and decided to bat

England 288 (J H Edrich 62, D Steele 73, A Greig 51 not out; G Gilmour 6-85) and 291 (D Steele 92). Australia 135 (P Edmonds 5-28) and 220-3 (RB McCosker 95; IM Chappell 62)

MATCH DRAWN* abandoned due to vandalism of pitch

August, 1977:

England won toss and decided to bat

England 436 (G Boycott 191, APE Knott 57). Australia 103 (IT Botham 5-21) and (following on) 248 (RW Marsh 63.

ENGLAND WON BY AN INNINGS AND 85 RUNS

July, 1981:

Australia won the toss and decided to bat

Australia 401-9 declared (J Dyson 102, KJ Hughes 89, GN Yallop 58; IT Botham 6-95) and 111 (RGD Willis 8-43). England 174 (IT Botham 50) and 356 (IT Botham 149 not out, G Dilley 56; TW Alderman 6-135).

ENGLAND WON BY 18 RUNS

June, 1985:

Australia won toss and decided to bat

Australia 331 (AMJ Hilditch 119) and 324 (AMJ Hilditch 80, KC Wessels 64, WB Phillips 91; JB Emburey 5-82). England 533 (RT Robinson 175, MW Gatting 53, IT Botham 60, PR Downton 54) and 123-5

ENGLAND WON BY FIVE WICKETS

June, 1989:

England won toss and decided to field

Australia 601-7 declared (MA Taylor 136, DM Jones 79, AR Border 66, SR Waugh 177 not out, MG Hughes 71) and 230-3 declared (MA Taylor 60, AR Border 60 not out). England 430 (KJ Barnett 80, AJ Lamb 125, RA Smith 66; TM Alderman 5-107) and 191 (GA Gooch 68; TM Alderman 5-44)

AUSTRALIA WON BY 210 RUNS

July, 1993:

Australia won toss and decided to bat

Australia 653-4 declared (DC Boon 107, AR Border 200 not out, SR Waugh 157 not out). England 200 (MA Atherton 55, GA Gooch 59; PR Reiffel 5-65) and (following on) 305 (MA Atherton 63, AJ Stewart 78)

AUSTRALIA WON BY AN INNINGS AND 148 RUNS

July, 1997:

Australia won the toss and decided to field

England 172 (JN Gillespie 7-37) and 268 (N Hussian 105, JP Crawley 72; PR Reiffel 5-49). Australia 501 (MTG Elliott 199, RT Ponting 127, PR Reiffel 54 not out; D Gough 5-149).

AUSTRALIA WON BY AN INNINGS AND 61 RUNS

August, 2001:

Australia won the toss and decided to bat

Australia 447 (RT Ponting 144, ME Waugh 72; DR Martyn 118; D Gough 5-103) and 176 for four declared (RT Ponting 72). England 309 (AJ Stewart 76 not out; GD McGrath 7-76) and 315-4 (MA Butcher 173 not out; N Hussian 55)

ENGLAND WON BY SIX WICKETS

ALSO AVAILABLE FROM GREAT NORTHERN BOOKS:

The Yorkshire County Cricket Club Yearbook

Relive every moment of Yorkshire County Cricket Club's season, meet all the players and get the lowdown on what it's like to be a professional cricketer for one of the most famous sporting clubs in history.

Bursting with facts and figures, the official yearbook of Yorkshire County Cricket Club is a detailed record of every match played in the season.

Featuring articles on players past and present, records from the history of Yorkshire Cricket and Internationals played at Headingley Carnegie, this book is essential reading for fans of Yorkshire cricket.

Sweet Summers
The Classic Cricket Writing of JM Kilburn
Winner of Wisden Book of the Year

Capturing a time when the true spirit of cricket existed. Some of the game's legends are brought to life including Donald Bradman, Fred Trueman, Jack Hobbs, Keith Miller, Garfield Sobers, Hedley Verity and Len Hutton. Kilburn is worth reading not only because he was a knowledgeable and respected interpreter of cricket, but also for the historical and social perspective.

Trueman's Tales
'Fiery Fred' – Yorkshire's Cricketing Giant
By John Morgan & David Joy
With contributions from: Dickie Bird, Ian Botham, Geoffrey Boycott, Brian Close, Raymond Illingworth, Bill Pertwee and Harvey Smith.

This book began as a collaboration between Fred Trueman and David Joy in early 2006. Then came Fred's untimely death. Sports journalist, and long-time friend of Fred Trueman, John Morgan, completed the book, which became a fitting tribute to a cricketing legend. Featuring the last recorded interviews with Fred, a collection of his humorous tales of life on and off the pitch, and tributes from many of his sporting colleagues and close friends. Illustrated throughout.

www.greatnorthernbooks.co.uk